WHERE HAVE ALL
THE PROPHETS GONE?

WHERE HAVE ALL THE PROPHETS GONE?

E. DEAN COOK

Xulon Press

Xulon Press
2301 Lucien Way #415
Maitland, FL 32751
407.339.4217
www.xulonpress.com

Edited by Xulon Press.

Printed in the United States of America.

ISBN-13: 9781545616055

CONTENTS

INTRODUCTION

A number of years ago while living in Monterey, California, I was assigned to provide chaplain coverage to a small Coast Guard group located on Highway 1 south at Big Sur. On my initial visit, I followed the scenic highway down the beautiful coast past Carmel-by-the-Sea. After several miles, the roadway began to wind high above the ocean along the jagged mountainside and eventually settled down into a flat stretch where cows lazily grazed in a large field alongside the road. At one end of the pasture next to the ocean stood a large, high rock formation atop of which stood an old lighthouse. The road leading up to the top had signs warning us, "Danger! Keep out! Absolutely no trespassing!" I called the Coast Guard, identified myself, and asked permission to visit the site. They warned me of the dangers but graciously granted me permission to climb the hill at my own risk.

Months later, I returned to climb the treacherous road up to the top. Upon reaching the lighthouse, I found that I had discovered a bit of California history. The lighthouse complex had been built atop this rocky promontory around 1889, during a period, which saw heavy maritime traffic up and down the California coast. The increase in shipping and the lack of experience on the part of captains sailing along this dangerous stretch of coast had put many a ship at risk. The shallow rocks extending out toward the shipping lanes, combined with high winds and rough seas, created a hazardous sailing area. The government, observing this problem, made a decision to build a lighthouse at this particular location because of its visibility far out at sea. For many years the lighthouse keeper and his family lived on this formidable site in a small stone house next to the beacon. However, at the time I made my visit to the site, it was run remotely by the Coast Guard.

This faithful lighthouse is much like the prophets of God who ministered throughout the history of Israel and the church. They often lived in lonely and dangerous places under difficult circumstances, and they served to warn others of spiritual dangers that could be fatal if certain paths were not abandoned. Today our nation and world stand in need of a clear beacon to shine into our treacherous night. The theme of this book laments the loss of the prophet's voice today and offers some concrete proposals on how we might recover this vital communication of alarm. In our study, we discuss the rise and fall of the Old Testament prophet in Israel's turbulent history. We then examine the role of the prophet John the Baptist and the Master Prophet, Jesus Christ, along with Jesus' warning about false prophets. A brief summary is presented of the prophets in church history as well as six contemporary views of the ministry of prophets today. Finally, a number of proposals are offered as practical ways of transforming the church today into more prophet-friendly congregations.

ACKNOWLEDGMENTS

I humbly acknowledge the Lord's hand throughout this project. I also owe a great debt to my devoted wife, Ruth, who helped prepare the manuscript and offered many invaluable suggestions to clarify and focus the message. My special appreciation to my sons, Scott, Todd, and Kevin. Scott introduced me to Eric Dolin's book on lighthouses, *Brilliant Beacons*, that inspired me to see God's prophets as beacons of divine light. Todd drew the lighthouse sketches and offered wise counsel from his own experience as a published author. Kevin, also a published writer, provided excellent direction on the publishing world.

Finally, my sincere thanks to two special friends who came alongside me in the final stages of preparation to offer their precious time and knowledge of literature and composition.

The contribution of all of these is sprinkled like gold dust over the entire text, making it more than I could ever have hoped to have done alone. I am deeply grateful to you all.

CHAPTER ONE

WHERE HAVE ALL THE PROPHETS GONE?

T he prophets lived in times of national, political, and religious upheavals, not unlike our own day. Our secular culture, courts, media, educational system, and government seem to have a grip on us like a giant python—and it is slowly squeezing the freedom, the hope, and the religious life out of many. Moral boundaries that stood for centuries, and in some cases millennia, are falling. A spokesperson for a historical evangelical church in a major city recently announced that the church had appointed two lesbian pastors, married to each other, to co-pastor their congregation. The spokesperson commented, "They are the best pastors we could find." The interpretation of that comment will be left to the reader. At the same time, a new level of vulgarity is polluting our language and our conversation as our public discourse has become more crude, harsh, and truth-free.

While people march in the streets, nations prepare for realignment, military budgets increase, and refugees flood the world, our future is becoming more and more uncertain. Meanwhile, in order to attract and hold worshippers, churches are restructuring their staffs, redecorating their sanctuaries, and dressing down, while turning the music volume up in worship services. They are busily expanding the coffee and breakfast bar while trying to avoid any mention of the words sin, guilt, or judgment. A megachurch pastor was heard reminding his congregation repeatedly, "You are not bad people; you are not bad people." While the darkness seems to be increasing, the beacons of God's truth seem to be decreasing. It makes one wonder: Where have all the prophets gone? Long time passing! Long time passing!

In 1955, on his way to Oberlin College, Pete Seeger pulled from his pocket the words of an old Cossack song that he had read in a book. The song was entitled, *"Koloda-Dudo."* Most of the world would never have heard it had he not added some words, put it to music, and later recorded the song. Over the next few years the song became a huge hit by the Kingston Trio. It was sung at folk gatherings all around the world and also won Seeger a Grammy. The name of the song? "Where Have All the Flowers Gone?" Actually, as popularized in the 1960s, it was a song protesting the Vietnam War. This writer first heard the song while en route to participate in that war. The words went something like this: "Where have all the flowers gone, long time passing. When will they ever learn, when will they ever learn?" The words lament the passing of our fine young men in battle, a tragedy I felt personally as I witnessed this loss of life first-hand.

Some of us feel this same sense of loss today by what appears to be the passing of our prophets. Where have they all gone, long time passing? When will we ever learn, when will we ever learn? Where are the Samuels, the Elijahs, the Jeremiahs, the Daniels, and the Pauls, who once shone so brightly? In the chapters that follow, we will examine the rise and the role of the biblical prophets, how they received their call, the content of their message, and how they delivered it faithfully. It is hoped that this study will forever enhance the reader's appreciation of these special beacons of God and their significant role in the church.

Lighthouses have long served an important function in the history of mankind, the first being built almost three hundred years before Christ at Alexandria, Egypt. The city, named after Alexander the Great, was to become the center and resource for the spread of Hellenistic teaching and culture throughout the ancient Mediterranean world. In order to transport this learning and commerce, the city needed a large seaport. As shipping increased sharply, so did the number of vessels entering and departing Alexandria's harbor.

This increase resulted in the loss of numerous vessels as they tried to navigate the narrow and shallow entrance to the harbor. In answer to this, the city made a major decision to construct a large lighthouse at the entrance of the harbor. It was destined to become one of the Seven Wonders of the Ancient World and was thought to stand nearly 450 feet high, with a large base constructed to withstand the most severe storms. On top of the tower stood a large cupola in which a bright fire burned twenty-four hours a day. The smoke from the lighthouse marked the entrance of the harbor by day, and its light shone as a beacon marking the harbor at night. This magnificent structure was a tribute to early architecture and engineering and stood for nearly a thousand years. This meant that it was standing during the time of Jesus' ministry upon the earth. The city gave the lighthouse the name, *Pharo.* A study of lighthouses today is known as *pharology.* The foundation of this ancient lighthouse has been discovered by archeologists.

Why call attention to this first man-made lighthouse? I do so because I believe that instead of *Pharo* it might well have been named *Prophet* because it was a powerful symbol of the light God's prophets brought to the world.

CHAPTER TWO

THE RISE OF PROPHETS

If we go back beyond the founding of Israel, we find that prophets existed in many cultures as valued members of a larger group of wise counselors. In addition to the prophets or seers, there were magicians or diviners, wise men, and priests. They had much in common, yet each had his own area of ministry. The prophets tended to stand outside the system and to offer their services to the community and its leaders. This included secular and spiritual counseling as well as communicating with the gods on their behalf. When God formed the Israelites into a separate people group, they welcomed the ministry of the wise men, the priests, and the prophets. However, the magicians and diviners were forbidden to counsel God's people because they were counterfeits who used deception.

God referred to Abraham, who is considered the father of the Hebrew race and nation, as a prophet (Genesis 20). When King Abimelech took Abraham's wife, Sarah, who Abraham had introduced as his sister, God appeared to the pagan king in a dream. Before he could violate her, God said to him, "I kept you from sinning against me . . . I did not let you touch her . . . Now return the man's wife for he is a prophet, so he will pray for you and you shall live. If you do not return her, know that you shall surely die and all who are yours" (Genesis 20:6–7). This passage is important because it is the first time in

5

scripture that God used the term *prophet*, and he took strong measures to protect that prophet. Notice also the extreme penalty God attached to any threats against his prophet—the penalty of death.

One Hebrew word for prophet is *nabbi* which comes from the Akkadean word *nabu* meaning to name, call, or proclaim. In Exodus 4:10, God calls Moses to be His mouthpiece or *nabbi*. Moses argues that he is not eloquent and thus not worthy to accept this high calling. God then asks him the question, "Who made your mouth?" Then He answered Himself with, "It is I, the Lord" (Genesis 4:11). This is followed by God's assurance that, "I will be your mouth and will teach you what you should speak" (v. 12). God was angry over Moses' refusal to be His prophet or mouthpiece but finally settled for a compromise. Moses would be God's prophet, receiving God's Word. He would then speak it to his brother, Aaron, who would in turn speak it to the people. In this manner Moses remained God's prophet, though the people receive the message from Aaron. Over time, Moses' confidence as a speaking prophet grew and the need for Aaron's voice faded.

Exodus 20:18 records a second step in the development of the Hebrew prophet. Soon after the Exodus, Moses led the people to the foot of Mount Sinai where God spoke to him. There God displayed His power by shaking the mountain and bathed it in thunder. Flashes of lightning and the sound of trumpets were also heard. The Bible says the people stood afar off, afraid and trembling, saying to Moses, "You speak to us and we will listen, but do not let God speak to us lest we die." Again, God consented to their request, leaving Moses to act as His prophet and voice to the people.

The prophet's role is defined further by Moses:

> The Lord your God will raise up for you a prophet like me from among you, from your brothers—it is to him you are to listen—just as

you desired of the Lord your God at Horeb on the day of the assembly when you said, "Let me not hear again the voice of the Lord my God, or see this great fire any more, lest I die." And the Lord said to me, "They are right in what they have spoken. I will raise up for them a prophet like you from among their brothers. And I will put my words in his mouth and he shall speak to them all that I command them. And whoever will not listen to my words that he shall speak in my name, I myself will require it of him. But the prophet who presumes to speak a word in my name that I have not commanded him to speak, or who speaks in the name of other gods, that same prophet shall die." And if you say in your heart, "How may we know the word that the Lord has not spoken?"—when a prophet speaks in the name of the Lord, if the word does not come to pass or come true, that is a word that the Lord has not spoken; the prophet has spoken it presumptuously.

—Deuteronomy 18:15–22

This passage is well worth one's personal in-depth study because it not only defines for us more specifically who the prophet is but also speaks of the ultimate Prophet who would come in the form of Jesus Christ. Notice that it also issues a strong warning against false prophets. The true prophet was called to speak God's uncompromising, unalterable, and unvarnished truth, which often brought upon him the anger of his listeners.

Note also that in this passage Moses as prophet does both *forth telling* and *foretelling*. Other words used for prophet were *seer* or *Roeh* and sometimes *Hozeh*. Seer means not only forth telling but foretelling. Thus, we see an example of the prophet seeing into the future and speaking of those events.

Although Moses was a prophet, he was also the leader of the nation and its judge. Therefore, he was not exclusively a prophet but wore other hats. It is not until Samuel appears that we have a person called exclusively to be a prophet. He was born the son of a praying and devout woman, full of gratitude that God had given her a son. In response, she arranged to leave the boy with the senior priest at Shiloh, there to serve in the House of God. As a young man, Samuel was called by God to be a prophet.

One of the first assignments given Samuel was to carry a hard message to the priest who had befriended, raised, and mentored him. This senior priest, Eli, had two sons, Hophni and Phineas. The sons, although functioning as priests, were involved in immoral behavior. They had corrupted themselves as well as the worshippers and the sacred place. God directed Samuel to tell Eli that He was about to punish his house forever for the iniquity that Eli had known about and yet allowed. The iniquity was the sons' blasphemy against God, and Eli's guilt was that he failed to restrain it (I Samuel 3:13).

It is worth noting that age seems to have little to do with Samuel's call and direction. Samuel was the younger intern but was called by God to deliver a message of judgment to his own spiritual father. We can only imagine the emotional and spiritual trial for both Samuel and Eli. Dr. Andrew Blackwood, in his book *The Prophets,* reminds us that the prophets were greater than priests and kings. Because of Samuel's obedience to God in these difficult circumstances, God continued to anoint him with the Holy Spirit and use him as His voice. Samuel's exceptional integrity and loyalty to God set a high standard for future prophets. God would later call on him to anoint David as king—a king who at the peak of his reign would also be called to humble himself before a prophet.

<CHAPTER THREE>

MEN GREATER THAN KINGS

God reveals in scripture how He called and used His prophets to convey His message. In this chapter, we will look specifically at the prophetic ministry of Nathan and Elijah.

Nathan, the Storyteller

Nathan means *God has given.* He is the first prophet asked by God to speak a word of judgment and mercy to a king whom God has anointed over Israel. This must have been doubly hard for Nathan since the king was greatly loved and honored by the people. As a young lad David had become an instant hero when he killed Goliath, the Philistine who had cursed Israel.

After David was catapulted into national prominence as a young warrior, King Saul selected him to play the harp to soothe the king's troubled mind. Later, when Saul became more and more paranoid and jealous of the young hero, David was forced to flee from the point of Saul's spear. This crisis only heightens the intrigue that surrounded David and increased the Israelites' adoration of their hero. Eventually, God rejected Saul as king and sent Samuel to anoint David, who was destined to unify the twelve tribes under his leadership at Jerusalem. As the years of his reign passed, David became lax in his religious practices and devotion to God—a dire warning to us all.

Chapter Three

11

We are told in II Samuel 11 and 12 that at the time when kings went out to war in the spring of the year, David did not go out as he normally did. This was a major mistake on his part. A word of caution here! We tend to think that what followed was all by chance. I do not think so. I believe David may have had his eye on the beautiful wife of one of his officers, a Hittite who lived nearby on the palace grounds.

As one who lived in military communities for many years, I observed an ugly practice that occurred whenever the warriors went off to war. Few talked about it openly, but it happened repeatedly. Whenever servicemen were deployed to sea or off to battle, some took advantage of the lonely wives who were left behind. It was not always the men who were at fault. Some of these wives went looking for companionship. The actions of these men and women often led to immorality, unfaithfulness, betrayal, and, sometimes, even violence and death.

I believe David did not go off to war because he was already tempted by Bathsheba and was looking for an opportunity to be with her. In turn she, probably aware of his interest, may well have exposed herself to his lustful eyes. At any rate, we know that David allowed Satan to enter into his life as he looked, lusted, and invited her into his bedroom. He probably did this repeatedly over the days that followed. At the very least, we know that a child was conceived from the relationship. Consequently, David panicked and concocted a cover-up plan.

The king ordered Uriah home from the battlefront, in the hope he would sleep with his wife, and David's secret sin would continue to be hidden. Uriah returned home, but, being a man of great honor, he would not allow himself to sleep with his wife while his men were in harm's way. David's carefully laid plan failed. He then committed a greater sin by ordering General Joab to assign Uriah to a battle location where he was likely to be killed. This plan initially appeared to work as Uriah was killed, and David was free to take Bathsheba as his wife.

Uriah was buried and David moved the pregnant widow into the palace to "care for her and the child." Publicly, it appeared that David was doing a good deed for a grieving and destitute widow, when in reality, he was covering a series of dark sins against God, his family, Uriah's family, General Joab, and the entire nation.

A full year passed, and it appeared that David had escaped the consequences of his sins. The child, a son, was born in good health. The king's subjects were probably unaware of the breech of integrity that had occurred in the palace. However, they would soon find out because God had a prophet—a beacon, a lighthouse that would now shine into that darkness, exposing all its ugliness. One can only imagine the personal trauma this caused Nathan the prophet as he became aware of the depth of his beloved king's transgressions. He must have been sick at heart and tempted to flee to the sea like Jonah. Many of us would have found it difficult, if not impossible, to deliver God's uncompromising judgment to the king.

The Bible does not tell us whether Nathan's encounter with David was public or private. It is possible that the prophet appeared before David on the occasion of the king's regularly-scheduled court day when he functioned as judge of the people. In any case, Nathan presented his problem for the king's judgment. Notice that Nathan did not come into David's presence in a contemptuous manner. Rather, he was respectful of the king's office and the significance of the truth he was about to reveal.

The prophet carefully confronted David by telling him a story or parable of a rich man who took from a poor man his only little ewe lamb. David, who was once a shepherd himself, could easily identify with the poor man's love and loss of his only little ewe lamb. He was outraged at the rich man's greed and lack of compassion. Isn't it interesting how we can so easily see the sin in other people while excusing our own? The king, now acting as judge, declared justice would be served only when the rich man paid back to the poor man four times what he took from him. This statement would come back to haunt him when he heard what he was going to pay for his evil deeds.

It was then that Nathan dropped the bomb: "Thou art the man!" The verbal sword of the prophet sank deep into David's heart before he ever saw it coming. We can imagine David with a startled look on his face, suddenly falling to his knees, brought down by the exposure of the sins he had so carefully hidden. Nathan continued to speak to David, relaying the words of God's judgment:

> I anointed you king over Israel and I delivered you out of the hand of Saul. And I gave you your master's house and your master's wives into your arms and gave you the house of Israel and Judah. And if this were too little, I would add to you as much more. Why have you despised the word of the Lord, to do what is evil in his sight? You have struck down Uriah the Hittite with the sword and have taken his wife to be your wife . . . Now, therefore, the sword shall never depart from your house because you have despised me . . . Behold I will raise up evil against you out of your own house. And I will take your wives before your eyes and give them to your neighbor, and he shall lie with your wives in the sight of this sun. For you did it secretly, but I will do this thing before all Israel and before the sun.
>
> —II Samuel 12:7–12

David then said to Nathan the prophet, "I have sinned against the Lord" (12:13a). Nathan replies, "The Lord also has put away your sin. You shall not die. Nevertheless, because by this deed you have utterly scorned the Lord, the child who is born to you shall die" (12:13b–14). The meeting appears to end abruptly as verse 15 then says, "Nathan went to his house." God, through his prophet Nathan, held nothing back from the king. The message was brutal but absolutely true. However, the prophet's words were not without mercy and grace for the repentant king. This passage is a profound example of how God's prophets can illuminate the hidden transgressions of our lives. Notice, also, that while God was intensely honest and promises harsh consequences for David's sins, He never-theless responded to his confession and gave him a hope of forgiveness, reconciliation, and further opportunity for service.

Some final observations: as mentioned above, after David confessed his sins, the Lord directed the prophet to say, "The Lord has put away your sins. You shall not die but the child who was born to you shall die." Here we see a clear reference to Christ who, in the future, would die as the innocent one for not only David's sins but ours as well. Some writers have painted the Old Testament prophets as little more than hornets who buzzed around Israel, stinging all they could find. Not true! Although their messages often begin with a hard sting, they are followed by the healing ointment of God's grace for those who will truly repent.

Elijah, the Prophet of Fire

No Old Testament prophet has captured the hearts and imagination of the Jews as does Elijah. During the Passover feast in Jewish homes, the door is left open for Elijah and usu-ally a place is set for him on the Pascal table along with an empty chair, should Elijah come to celebrate with them this year. Sometimes children are sent to the door to watch for his coming. When John the Baptist appeared in the likeness of an Old Testament prophet, some thought he was Elijah. Peter, James, and John were witnesses to the visitation of Moses and

Elijah with Jesus on Mount Transfiguration. No other prophet is mentioned more often in the New Testament than is Elijah.

In the mid-ninth century BC, David and Solomon's kingdom broke apart into two separate kingdoms, north and south. Omri led the kingdom in the north, made up of ten tribes, and known officially as Israel. He established his capital in Samaria, along with a worship center, so the people could be independent from Jerusalem and Judea. Since the Northern Kingdom was bordered on the west by Phoenicia, Omri arranged for his son and future king, Ahab, to marry the daughter of the king of Sidon in Phoenicia. How much love there was between Ahab and Princess Jezebel is not clear, but for better or worse, it bound the two countries together and spelled trouble for Israel.

Ahab seemed to find purpose by constantly battling his enemies round about while Jezebel focused her energies on introducing her false gods and faith into Israel. Her pagan gods, Baal and Asherah, were old Canaanite gods and objects of fertility worship. Jezebel took personal interest in propagating her faith, building centers of worship in Samaria. She constructed them next to and even inside worship centers dedicated to Jehovah. This allowed Israelites who came to worship their God to have the choice of worshipping the pagan gods of Jezebel also. In other words, those who were concerned with the success of their herds and crops could worship the true God *in spirit and in truth* or visit the pagan temple prostitutes who offered their services to help with fertility. It was common practice for some Israelites during this period to waver between two or more gods and forms of worship. Since they were unable to make up their minds as to who was the true god, they tried to appease the gods they thought would help them.

Since the Israelites had already weakened their faith by separating from Jerusalem and its temple and priesthood, the addition of Jezebel's sacred places only added confusion and weakness to their spiritual life. This crisis, which King Ahab did nothing to alleviate, gave rise to God's call for the prophet from Gilead whom we know as Elijah. This messenger was not one to sit back while everything disintegrated. The best defense is usually a good offense, and that is exactly what God did by calling Elijah to the attack.

In I Kings 18, the prophet delivered the first salvo to King Ahab himself in the form of a dire announcement. God was going to shut off the water for what turned out to be three-and-a-half years. If one wants to get the attention of a leader who rules over an arid land where water is already at a premium, he should simply announce that there will be no more rain until God speaks.

We are not told how Ahab immediately responded, but we assume that he took the words seriously and retired to his palace to consult with Jezebel. Meanwhile, Elijah departed, and God hid him for three-and-a-half years during the long drought. God first assigned him to a remote place by a stream on the other side of the Jordon River where he was miraculously fed by ravens as the drought deepened. The land grew parched, the crops dried up, the herds grew weak, and the people in the land all suffered from lack of water. Had Jezebel found Elijah during this time, she would almost certainly have killed him, but God's hand protected him from her. Toward the end of this period, God hid, the prophet in a widow's home in Jezebel's native Phoenicia.

At the end of the three-and-a-half years, the prophet of light again appears to King Ahab whose first response is to call Elijah "the troubler of Israel." It is an acknowledgment that the prophet had shaken the nation. Like King Ahab, we often want to put our faults and failures on other people. Elijah would not let him off so easily but replied that he, the king, is in fact "the troubler of Israel." However, the prophet had not come to argue that point; he had come to make a greater demand. He asked the king to gather Jezebel's prophets to Mount Carmel, along with the people of Israel, to view a contest that would determine who is the true God—Jehovah or Baal. The general rules were that each side was to build a public altar and pray. The god that answered by fire would prove to be the true God.

Mount Carmel was the perfect place for such a contest. It protrudes some 1500 feet above the flat land and provides a view all the way to the Mediterranean. How long it took for the invitation to spread across the kingdom and for the general public to gather, we do not know; but we do know that Ahab and Jezebel's nearly 900 false prophets showed up for the contest. It is inferred that Ahab was present but not Jezebel. Elijah assumed leadership of the event by addressing the people, "How long will you go limping between two different opinions? If the Lord is God, follow Him; but if Baal, then follow him" (I Kings 18:21–22). The Bible says the people did not answer him a word. Apparently, they could not make up their minds yet, or they were all out of breath from climbing the mountain.

Then Elijah announced the start of the contest by inviting the prophets of Baal to go first. They built their altar, prepared their sacrifice, and prayed their prayers, but no fire fell. The prophet extended their opportunity by giving them overtime minutes just to be fair. In the meantime, he chided them, suggesting that their god or gods might be on a trip somewhere or busy in the bathroom. Jezebel's prophets tried again with more enthusiasm and earnestness, even cutting themselves and crying out in desperation—but still no fire!

Elijah then stepped forth at the hour of the daily evening sacrifice and asked the people to come near. Elijah repaired the altar of the Lord that had been neglected and thrown down—a picture of their faith. Taking twelve stones, according to the number of tribes, he rebuilt the altar. The purpose of this was to remind the Israelites that they were really a part of a greater nation. After putting wood on the altar and preparing the sacrifice, the attendants were asked to fill four jars with water to pour on the altar, the wood, and the sacrifice. This was repeated three times until even the trench surrounding the altar was overflowing.

An obvious question that comes to mind is, "Where did they get the water?" I think I discovered the answer while living in Honolulu, Hawaii. Located in the mountains above the city are massive natural reservoirs that contain water. Perhaps there were similar natural reservoirs in Mount Carmel, and that was one of the reasons God chose this location for the contest. Further research could be done geologically on this issue.

The timing of Elijah's sacrifice is important since, as noted above, it took place at the temple's usual time of evening worship. By choosing this time, he was appealing to the Israelites' remembrance of their historic national and religious life. Elijah stepped forth and prayed:

> O, Lord, God of Abraham, Isaac and Israel, let it be known this day that you are God in Israel, and that I am your servant, and that I have done all these things at your word. Answer me, O Lord, answer me, that this people may know that you, O Lord, are God, and that you have turned their hearts back.
> —I Kings 18:36–37

Instantly the fire of the Lord fell, consuming the offering, the wood, the stones, the dust, and even the water in the trench! It must have been a frightening moment as those present felt the heat against their skin and wonder how near it may come to them.

When the people saw this incredible phenomenon, they fell on their faces and cried out, "The Lord is God! The Lord is God!" Elijah then asked the people to seize the prophets of Baal and kill them all, which they did. After this he said to King Ahab, "Go up! Eat and drink, for there is a sound of rushing rain." Ahab raced to the city of Jezreel to tell Jezebel all that Elijah had done and how he had killed all the prophets of Baal. Jezebel was angry and threatened to kill the prophet. However, Elijah would survive, and in the days ahead, he would announce the death of both King Ahab and Queen Jezebel. In death they would both *go to the dogs* as ferocious canines devoured Jezebel and licked Ahab's life blood—a powerful picture of the detestable leaders they had become. Elijah would later be caught up into Heaven in a fiery chariot pulled by fiery horses. This one-of-a-kind ascension into Heaven only added to the mystery of this powerful prophet and is something of a picture of Christ's own ascension into Heaven.

What did God accomplish through this beacon of light, the prophet Elijah? It is believed that many of the Israelites did turn back to God that day when they saw the divine fire fall and heard the courageous prophet challenge them to choose and follow the true God. Courage is always contagious.

Why did God spare Elijah the experience of death by taking him directly to Heaven? Could the reason be that he had already died a thousand deaths when he chose to oppose King Ahab and Queen Jezebel? We don't know the answer for sure. What we do know is that the obedience of this prophet ended the evil line of the house of Omri. Elijah's words of obedience gave the Israelites the opportunity to rethink their sinful ways and turn back to God before it was too late. Sometimes that is all prophets can do. They can open a door and provide a way of escape, but they cannot make anyone walk through it.

CHAPTER FOUR

GOLDEN AGE OF THE PROPHETS

Isaiah, the Prophet of Salvation

In 1611 France built its first lighthouse. It is 223 feet high and located at the mouth of the Gironde estuary in south-western France, not far from the port city of Bordeaux. Some say it is more like a palace than a lighthouse, and it is often called the Versailles of the Sea. It actually has a king's chamber built into it, although no king has ever been known to stay there. Richly decorated throughout with marble, it also contains a gilded chapel with four stained-glass windows and beautiful sculptures. Although the lighthouse has been refined, it is still a lighthouse, and with later improvements in lighting and lenses, it surpasses all lighthouses built in America. Called the Cordouan Lighthouse, it could be likened to the prophet Isaiah who did not display the roughness of some of the other prophets but was an educated, refined, and gifted preacher and writer. Because of his special gifts, his light shone further, clearer, and in more directions than did that of most of the other prophets. In the end, however, Isaiah was still just a trusted lighthouse for God.

Isaiah is probably the most beloved prophet of the Christian Church. He lived in Jerusalem around the mid-eighth century BC, a time when his nation was entering its crucial period of darkness. His ministry spanned the reigns of at least five kings: Jotham, Uzziah, Ahaz, Hezekiah, and Manasseh. The book that bears his name falls easily into two sections. The first focuses on the doom that will befall Judah for her sins, her empty religious rituals, and her alliances with foreign governments. The second section deals primarily with hope and contains the wonderful Messianic passages regarding the eternal kingdom to come.

Isaiah's call is unique, and he spent some time giving us the details. In Chapter 6 of his book, he tells us that this account took place in the year that King Uzziah died. The king had been smitten with leprosy when he foolishly assumed duties that belonged to the priesthood alone. His death threw the country into turmoil. Isaiah, in grief, entered the temple to pray, and while there was given a powerful vision of God. The vision portrayed in Chapter 6 reveals God high and lifted up, sitting on His throne as seraphim worship Him and cry, "Holy! Holy! Holy is the Lord God of Hosts. The whole earth is full of His glory."

This vision was probably given to Isaiah so he would understand that although the king had died, the world had not ended. God was still their king. As he continued to watch the vision, he became a broken man, crying out, "Woe is me for I am lost; for I am a man of unclean lips, for my eyes have seen the King, the Lord of Hosts." A seraph then brought a burning coal to Isaiah and touched his lips saying, "Your guilt is taken away and your sins atoned for." Following Isaiah's cleansing and pardon, God asked him a direct question, "Who will go for us?" Isaiah replied, "Here am I. Send me!" God now directed the prophet to go speak to the people. This calling, which Isaiah shares with us, might serve as a model for the calling of all prophets, pastors, and missionaries: it is clear, it is profound, it is serious, and it is urgent.

The first task God gave the prophet is to go to King Ahaz with a critical message. Like Samuel, Nathan, and Elijah, Isaiah was asked to confront the most powerful person in the kingdom. His message was related to the rising Assyrian empire to the north which wanted to swallow up Judah. The prophet was asked to warn the king of Judah not to form an alliance with Syria but to trust God for salvation and security. The king listened to the prophet but rejected God's Word and proceeded to make an alliance with his enemy. When Ahaz discovered his mistake he made a second alliance with Egypt against Assyria, stubbornly refusing to hear the prophet and trust God for national safety.

Assyria invaded Judah because they did not trust the king. Since Israel was no match for Assyria's 140,000-man army, Isaiah pleaded again with the king to fear God and wait for Him (Isaiah 8:11ff.). King Ahaz, who was greatly outnumbered, could do nothing else. While the Assyrian army encamped in preparation for the coming battle, an angel of the Lord moved throughout the camp at night, and the invading army mysteriously died. When Assyria's King Sennacherib realized his devastating loss, he flew from Judah and returned to Nineveh. Notice that Isaiah was not God's mouthpiece only on a one-time basis, but rather, he returned repeatedly to advise the king of God's will. For the sake of Israel and His name, God honored the prophet's persistence and saved His people in spite of their disobedient king.

Some scholars believe that Isaiah's ministry ended prematurely when he was sawed in two by King Manassas, who despised him, and that another writer actually finished the last half of the book. Others believe, as does this writer, that the entire book belongs to Isaiah as it reflects his spirit, his intellect, and his writing style. Jesus quoted the book in Mark 11:17, giving Isaiah full credit by saying, "Is it not written, 'My house shall be called a House of Prayer for all nations but you have made it a den of thieves'" (Isaiah 56:7). Again, in Matthew 15:7, Jesus said to His critics:

> For the sake of tradition you have made void the Word of God, you hypocrites! Well did Isaiah prophesy of you when he said, "The people honor me with their lips but their heart is far from me; in vain do they worship me, teaching as doctrines the commandments of men."

St. Mark also began his Gospel of Jesus Christ by quoting the prophet:

> The beginning of the Gospel of Jesus Christ, the Son of God. As it is written in Isaiah the Prophet, "Behold I send my messenger before your face who will prepare your way. The voice of one crying in the wilderness; 'Prepare the way of the Lord, make His paths straight.'"

Isaiah and Mark were both speaking of Christ and John the Baptist, who was sent to prepare His way. Thus, Jesus and the New Testament writers validated the inspiration of Isaiah's prophesy.

Jeremiah, the Weeping Prophet

Near Key Largo, Florida, a great reef extends out into the sea. Between 1830 and 1860, scores of ships met their fate on this submerged reef. The great loss led to a study of how to protect the ships that sailed these waters. A lighthouse seemed to be the best answer, so the Army Corps of Engineers did a study to determine the design. The chosen structure was to stand on eight legs in four feet of water. The legs would be screwed into the sand; then large cast-iron disks would be slid down onto the legs, forming a second sea bed on which to stabilize the lighthouse. The lighthouse and the keeper's residence were built high above the water on the open legs. The lantern

26

room itself was built on the very top of this unusual structure. The strange-looking lighthouse was soon given the name *The Skeleton Tower*. The lighthouse was located in a storm center. It often endured high winds and waves of hurricane force. It was a tough mission for a lighthouse, but by shining in the darkness, it succeeded in saving many a ship and its crew from loss.

Jeremiah was called of God to serve as a lighthouse at the center of a storm. His whole ministry would be spent in the hurricane of Judah's final years as a nation. In spite of extreme difficulty, Jeremiah was faithful and continued to shine into the darkness to the very end. As a child, I remember when my family traveled from Missouri to California in the early 1950s. What impressed me most was that upon leaving Missouri's green hills, trees, ponds and streams, we found ourselves driving across the brown plains of Kansas. The prairies seemed to me to be mile upon mile of dreary landscape, interrupted only by occasional telephone poles, railroad tracks, or service stations. Some people see Jeremiah's books (Jeremiah and Lamentations) as the same kind of landscape. It can seem like chapter after chapter of repetition and lament with little to make the heart sing. Some have said they read Jeremiah only as an act of penance. However, truth is not always happy, is it? Sometimes truth is sad, painful, and disappointing. We can learn from God's unpleasant truth also.

Jeremiah served from about 627 BC in Judah under Josiah the king, who had been crowned ruler at age eight. Remarkably, he grew up to be a good king and a reformer, ridding most of the nation of idolatry. Upon his death, however, the kings who followed allowed the national sins to return with even more abandonment. When King Jehoiakim foolishly rebelled against King Nebuchadnezzar of Babylon, the Babylonian king invaded Judah, killed the king, and took his son along with 10,000 Hebrews into exile. When the king who succeeded Jehoiakim also rebelled against Babylon, Nebuchadnezzar returned with a vengeance, destroying the city and the temple, leaving only a remnant of the people behind.

It was during this period when Judah was in conflict with Babylon that God called Jeremiah to prophesy. He urged the people to repent and return to God, in hopes of avoiding complete destruction of the nation. However, most of his listeners despised him, persecuted him, and imprisoned him, even burning his writings. They chose rather to listen to the false prophets who told them not to worry, that all would be well. Jeremiah's words, which God gave him directly, proved to be absolutely true and he never wavered from them. Sometimes a prophet's message will not be heard at the time, but that is no reason for him to be silent. Time will always honor God's Word. Even after their nation's destruction, false prophets continued telling the people not to worry since they would be home soon.

Jeremiah, however, sent them letters to correct this false prophesy and told them to expect an exile period of up to seventy years. This was emotionally devastating to the exiles and robbed them of any hope of seeing their beloved nation again.

Jeremiah had neither the eloquence nor the writing skills of Isaiah, but his messages were no less true and urgent. His obedience to his call, his courage to stand against all odds, and his willingness to suffer great personal loss qualified him as one of the great prophets and a role model—even today. Too many pastors are tempted give up when things get hard, but that is when they are needed the most.

So, why is Jeremiah called the Weeping Prophet? Was it that he felt sorry for himself, for his failure, or the ridicule of his tormenters? No! Jeremiah wept over Jerusalem because he had the heart of Christ; Christ Himself would also weep over Jerusalem before He died. Jeremiah could not sing or smile over the sin of his nation. Andrew Blackwood, renowned preacher of the early 1900s, once said, "The man who smiles over his country's sin is a traitor." Jeremiah was no traitor.

Ezekiel, the Prophet in Exile

Thomas Carlyle, the Scottish philosopher, historian, writer, and naturalist who lived in the mid-1800s, wrote about a very unusual lighthouse found on a South Sea island. A certain large insect of the island, when wounded, gave off a small light in its agony. The natives, according to Carlyle, would spear the insects and hold them over their heads to light their way through the dark jungle—light coming from suffering. God chose Ezekiel to be a beacon of light through his own suffering. Sometime around 597 BC, he was carried away with the exiles from Jerusalem to Babylon. As he made this march of tears with his countrymen and their families, he no doubt passed through the valley where Israel had fought her last battle. If so, he would have seen the carnage of the unburied bodies of the Hebrews and Babylonians. Scattered bones covered the field of battle. As they made their long march on to Babylon, Ezekiel would have experienced and seen great suffering, death, grief, and the burial of those who were unable to complete the march.

Upon reaching Babylon, the exiles were given small plots of land outside the city, on which to till and provide for their own welfare. They were not made slaves by the Babylonians, but they enslaved themselves in their anger, grief, and loss. It was into this environment that God called Ezekiel to be a prophet of hope to the hopeless. Jesus' words spoken in Matthew 6:23 say that "If the light in you is darkness, how great is the darkness." When God calls Ezekiel, He speaks honestly from his heart concerning the disloyalty of the people:

> And He said to me, "Son of Man, stand on your feet, and I will speak to you." And as He spoke to me, the Spirit entered into me and set me on my feet, and I heard Him speaking to me. And He said to me, "Son of Man, I send you to the

people of Israel, to nations of rebels, who have rebelled against me. They and their fathers have transgressed against me to this day. The descendants are impudent and stubborn: I send you to them and you shall say to them, 'Thus says the Lord God.' And whether they hear or refuse to hear (for they are a rebellious house), they will know that a prophet has been among them. And you, Son of Man, be not afraid of them, nor be afraid of their words, though briers and thorns are with you and you sit on scorpions. Be not afraid of their words, nor be dismayed at their looks, for they are a rebellious house. And you shall speak my words to them, whether they hear or refuse to hear for they are a rebellious house. But you, Son of Man, hear what I say to you. Be not rebellious like that rebellious house; open your mouth and eat what I give you."

—Ezekiel 2:1–8

God considered it important that the prophet He called have a clear assessment of the people to whom he is sent. It was not a rosy picture. Is there not an important lesson here as we prepare prophets, pastors, and missionaries today? Are we guilty of painting a too idealistic or romantic view of their task? Few pastors have ever been called to a church so harshly described as rebellious, obstinate, briers, thorns, and scorpions. Yet Ezekiel accepted that call without any assurance of success. This alone should qualify him as a great prophet.

Ezekiel was a young man, no more than twenty-five years of age, when he went into exile. God's message to Ezekiel complemented Jeremiah's message in preparing the people for a long stay. Judah needed to accept responsibility for her calamity but this would take time. The prophet's first challenge was to get the attention of the depressed and grieving exiles. In order to do so, he employed a number of unusual and creative means to illustrate the words of his message. For example, he lay on his side for 390 consecutive days, to awaken the people to the reality of the loss of Jerusalem and the suffering of their brothers and sisters. On another occasion, he limited his diet to twelve ounces of bread and two pints of water a day, to emphasize the starvation of the Hebrews when Jerusalem was under siege. Ezekiel was so focused on getting his message to the people that he refused to engage in ordinary conversation but limited his speech to the words of God only. To call attention to the great loss of the nation, he shaved his head and beard and burned the hair publicly to demonstrate the fires that burned in Jerusalem.

Later, Ezekiel turned from the focus on grief to new visions regarding the restoration of the land, the temple, and the priesthood, as well as the coming righteous prince who would teach them God's truth and establish justice in the land again. It is a powerful picture of the coming Messiah. We see in Ezekiel a determined, compassionate, and creative prophet, able to adapt to his environment.

So, what can we learn from Ezekiel? (1) He is like a chap-lain-prophet in that he went where his people went: living, suffering, and grieving with them and being God's presence among them; (2) Ezekiel was willing to lay aside his own dignity, welfare, and reputation in order that that he might communicate God's love and hope to his countrymen; (3) Ezekiel also confronted the false prophets who sowed confusion, replacing their false hope with true teaching; and (4) He is a courageous and loving prophet.

Daniel, the Statesman Prophet

The Statue of Liberty was erected in the mid-1880s on Liberty Island in New York City Harbor. The Frenchman Frederic Auguste Bartholde designed the famous statue not only as a monument of friendship between the two nations, France and America, but also as a lighthouse, welcoming the world to our shores. The torch in Lady Liberty's hand was designed to hold nine carbon arc lamps that were to shine through holes cut in the metal flame. However, the light proved to be too dim as a navigational aid, causing a prominent New York publisher to call it a glowworm. Experimentation was begun to increase the visibility of the light, but it became apparent that the statue's design did not lend itself to the requirements of a traditional lighthouse.

President Teddy Roosevelt finally acknowledged this truth and signed the official papers that dropped the statue's function as a navigational aid, leaving it simply as a monument of friendship. Although it was no longer an official beacon light, its presence was still a powerful symbol that welcomed strangers to our shores. In a similar manner, Daniel did not fit the traditional mold of a prophet since he was actually a statesman, but his presence in key positions allowed God to use him as a divine messenger.

As a lad of no more than fourteen to seventeen years of age, Daniel was chosen by the conquering Babylonians to be trained in their government service and the culture, arts, language, and leadership of the Babylonian Empire. Along with his close friends, all of whom were probably of noble birth with great intellectual and leadership promise, Daniel grew up during the reign of the good Judean king Josiah. The strong spiritual foundation and piety reflected in this king's reign at the time must have greatly affected and influenced Daniel and his friends. In addition to the king's positive role model, Daniel was very likely impacted by the prophets Isaiah, Jeremiah, and Ezekiel. Even though these godly young men found themselves at the center of a pagan empire and culture, they nevertheless were determined to neither neglect nor compromise their faith in God—a powerful stand for such young men!

Miraculously, in the midst of all this corruption and temptation they managed, with God's help, to remain pure and grow in their professional reputations. What a lesson for young people today who are tempted to compromise with the world to get ahead. These young men of piety not only survived in the secular world but prospered in it, becoming valuable assets to Nebuchadnezzar's empire. As time went on, God used Daniel to speak His word not only to Nebuchadnezzar but also later to Darius and Cyrus, leaders of the Persian Empire that followed. Daniel's reputation for wisdom was apparently known throughout the Empire and beyond. Ezekiel speaks of Daniel in his own book as being renowned and admired for his wisdom and knowledge.

At the same time, while Daniel served a pagan emperor he still spoke publicly of God as the ruler over all as well as the revealer of Truth. He also declared God to be the Redeemer of Israel and of all people. Apparently he was not hobbled by political correctness. God gave him a number of important visions. Some of the most prominent of these visions are:

1. The Great Statue

    God gave Nebuchadnezzar a vision, which troubled the king greatly but which could not be interpreted by his wise men. Daniel was called upon to interpret the vision for the king The statue, God revealed to Daniel, represented four different Gentile empires that would come upon the earth—the first being Babylon. The last empire would be smashed by a large stone that would, in turn, become a mountain or a great kingdom filling the whole earth. We believe this stone to be Christ who will reign supreme at the end of the age.

2. The Seventy Weeks

This second vision was given to Daniel and contains the prophetic clock of seventy weeks or
490 years. God revealed to Daniel that during
this future time period, Jerusalem would be
rebuilt and the Messiah would come, only to
be cut off. Later the Tribulation would come
and Christ would return to the earth, this time
to rule supreme. No other prophet dealt with
such an astounding breadth of history and
events as did Daniel.

3. The Coming Antichrist

Finally, Daniel's prophecies in chapters 7-12
described the coming antichrist. This demonic
ruler dominates the earth for a time, claiming
to be God but is ultimately defeated by Christ.
The antichrist is killed and thrown into the fiery
pit. Then Daniel tells us:

He told me and made known to me the interpretation of the things, " . . . and the kingdom
and the dominion and the greatness of the kingdoms under the whole heaven shall be given to
the people of the saints of the Most High; his
kingdom shall be an everlasting kingdom and
all dominions shall serve and obey him." And
this is the end of the matter.
—Daniel 7:16b, 27–28a

Daniel is perhaps God's most powerful lighthouse with
the exception of Jesus, for Daniel's light shines all the way
from Babylon to the end of human history as we know it.

Daniel never forgot his people, and his influence was seen in Cyrus's decree which released the Jews to go back and restore their homeland:

> Thus says Cyrus, King of Persia. "The Lord, the God of heaven, has given me all the kingdoms of the earth, and he has charged me to build him a house at Jerusalem, which is in Judah. Whoever is among you of all his people, may his God be with him, and let him go up to Jerusalem, which is in Judah, and rebuild the house of the Lord, the God of Israel—He is the God who is in Jerusalem. And let each survivor, in whatever place he sojourns, be assisted by the men of his place with silver and gold, with goods and with beasts, besides freewill offerings for the house of God that is in Jerusalem."
>
> —Ezra 1:2–4

Some would say that Cyrus did this purely from a political motive. However, we know better. The spirit of Daniel can be seen throughout the decree. It is possible that he may have written it for the king's signature.

So what can we learn from Daniel? First, we do not have to abandon our faith to serve God in the secular world. Indeed, God has such a place for some of us, and we need to accept it as our ministry. Second, the secular world often has as much need of our piety as of our skills. Third, we see a gracious spirit in Daniel, whatever his situation. He never showed fear, anxiety, desperation, or anger. Even in the lion's den, his faith had a dignity about it, allowing him to pray with calm assurance that God's purposes would prevail. Historians tell us that Daniel died at the ripe old age of ninety, a princely statesman-prophet buried, we assume, in Babylon.

CHAPTER FIVE

DESCENDING INTO THE NIGHT

T he return of the exiles under the Persian king Cyrus was a time of rejoicing, but restoring the nation was not going to be an easy task. God sent three prominent prophets to assist the restoration. Their names were Haggai, Zechariah, and Malachi. Haggai encouraged the people to rebuild the temple; Zechariah gave the nation a vision of their role as a light before the world; and Malachi urged the priests to live lives of integrity and holiness before the people they served, in addition to teaching God's Word.

One would like to report that the people heard the Word of God gladly and that Israel experienced a great spiritual revival, becoming a beacon of hope to the world. Sad to say, it did not happen. They limped on into the darkness where they remained for nearly four hundred years. As the Old Testament period drew to a close, the people became more and more content with their darkness. Although not a lot was happening with the Israelites during this period, there was plenty happening in the Gentile world, and this would greatly affect the Hebrew people.

For example, Rome, a civilization that had been founded around 753 BC as a loose collection of villages, each with their own king, was now expanding. By 265 BC Rome had become a powerful republic that ruled over all the Italian peninsula.

Rome sought to expand eastward; however, Carthage, a powerful Phoenician kingdom and Mediterranean shipping giant, stood in her way. In 146 BC, Rome was able to defeat Carthage, opening the way for her legions to march into Asia Minor and the Middle East. As the dominos fell, Rome extended her reach all the way to Syria and Palestine by 6 BC. Also by that time, Rome was no longer a republic but an empire that ruled the world—including the nation and people of Israel.

It was the practice of Rome to grant a certain amount of local sovereignty to nations it had conquered, even allowing them to use their own currency. This also included extending religious freedom to conquered people as long as peace was maintained. Rome assigned Philip the Tetrarch to rule northern Palestine. He proved to be a just and fair ruler of the Jews. Herod the Great was crowned king of the Jews in 40 BC, and twenty years later, he undertook a major building and renovation program in Jerusalem, which included the expansion of the temple. This temple project would take nearly eighty years to complete. Herod's temple was constructed of white marble, much of it overlaid with gold. It was a spectacular sight as the sun reflected against its walls and pillars.

Herod also reinstated the priestly office. He located their quarters between the temple's great porticos. The beautiful sanctuary was surrounded by a series of courts: the Priests' Court, the Women's Court, the Israelites' Court, the Gentiles' Court, and an outer court. It took twelve steps to ascend from the court into the sanctuary itself. The Holy of Holies was hidden by a very thick, ornate curtain. However, the sacred inner sanctum itself was empty. The Ark of the Covenant that had earlier resided in this sacred space had been lost or destroyed during the time of the Babylonian destruction of Jerusalem. The emptiness of the Holy of Holies in many ways was a symbol of the spiritual emptiness of God's people.

During the intertestamental period, approximately 250 BC, religious books began to be written that were of interest to the Jews and later to the church. They were called apocryphal writings which meant *hidden things.* Some of these books, of unknown origin and of questionable inspiration, were retained by the Jews and some Christians. They had no authority in the church, but some church leaders viewed them as profitable for study. The Roman Catholic Church placed them in their Bible between the Old Testament and the New, as did the early versions of the Protestant King James Bible. However, over time, the Protestants deleted them. The Roman Catholics still use the apocryphal books in worship. Below is a list of selected apocryphal books:

Title	Approximate Date Written
Letter to Jeremiah	317 BC
Tobit	250–175 BC
Baruch	200 BC–AD 70
Ecclesiasticus (Sirach)	190 BC
Judith	175–110 BC
Songs of the Three Children	167–163 BC
I Esdras	150 BC
Bel and the Dragon	150–100 BC
Prayer of Manasseh	150–50 BC
Wisdom of Solomon	150 BC–AD 40
I Maccabees	63–10 BC
II Maccabees	100 BC
Susanna	100 BC
II Esdras	70–135 AD

There were also thirteen or more pseudepigraphical writings that the church did not include in the canon because their origin could not be authenticated. Nevertheless, they are considered by scholars as a source of perhaps some reliability during this period of history. These writings include:

Title	Approximate Date Written
Enoch	200–63 BC
Letter of Aristeas	170–130 BC
Book of Jubilees	150–100 BC
Testaments of Twelve Patriarchs	130 BC
III and IV Maccabees	1 BC
Sibylline Oracles	80 BC–AD 130
Psalms of Solomon	40 BC
Book of Adam and Eve	AD 1
Lives of the Prophets	AD 1
Assumption of Moses	AD 1–30
II Baruch	AD 70–100
Ascension of Isaiah	AD 2

This literature may contain some prophetic truth, but it could also contain some fiction and forgeries. It is wise for the student to focus on the canonical record of the prophets whose origins and lives are well documented.

CHAPTER SIX

THE MASTER
PROPHET — JESUS

rophets of the Old Testament were a dynamic and powerful voice for God. The goal of all prophets and prophesy was the holiness of God, a holiness that would one day be demonstrated by the coming Christ and, through Him, would be made effectual for all who believed in Him. The coming Christ was the heart of all prophecy. They agreed in their inspired messages that righteousness exalts a nation, and sin will destroy it. These messages all pointed to the future when the matchless and master prophet would come to fulfill these hopes and dreams of a righteous kingdom. The prophets did not live in a cloister or an academic world or a walled Vatican. They lived with and among the people, carrying their pain, their burdens, and their disappointments, but they also carried a steady light into their darkness. This light was both timely and timeless. While the world often tried to quiet them, they would not be silenced. When they ceased to speak, the culture and the people suffered, and the world grew dark.

The prophets' long silence during the intertestamental period was finally broken by two unassuming prophets whom God had led to the Temple to make an astounding discovery and announcement. Simeon and Anna, a prophet and prophetess, were present when Mary and Joseph brought the Christ child to the temple to make a thank offering to God on behalf of His birth.

As the shy couple made their way anonymously through the crowd, they were startled by the sudden appearance of Simeon who intercepted them. Luke, in chapter two, records that the prophet recognized the divine nature of the child they carried and asked to take the baby into his arms. Doing so, he blessed God and prophesied in the presence of temple worshippers: "My eyes have seen your salvation that you have prepared in the presence of all people." These worshippers were greatly honored to be the first to see the Christ child come to His holy temple. This was not the usual way someone of such importance was introduced, but God seldom does things the usual way. One can only imagine how overwhelmed Joseph and Mary must have felt, not knowing what the revelation would mean.

They had not gone much further when they were accosted again, this time by the prophetess Anna who also recognized the Christ child. Anna burst into spontaneous thanksgiving before God and the people. She also prophesied publicly, saying that this child is the one for whom they have been waiting to redeem Jerusalem. This incident was profound yet so low-key that we are apt to pass over it. No priest or scribe or rabbi is mentioned as recognizing the child, although they must have been present or nearby. Neither is the response of the crowd of worshippers mentioned. We should not be surprised since people often hear profound things in a church service, yet do not immediately respond to them.

Several observations can be made here: first, God saw to it that the Christ child was revealed in the house of worship and, second, that He was introduced by prophets, both a man and a woman. Finally, the description of the incident indicates that Joseph and Mary did not seek in any way to exploit the occasion or use it for personal gain.

As Jesus grew up quietly in His hometown of Nazareth, we can assume that He knew and perhaps interacted occasionally with His cousin John, at least on their annual pilgrimage to Jerusalem for Passover. John was six months older and was destined to play a critical role in preparing the nation for Jesus' appearance and coming ministry. Cousin John had traded his family priesthood role for a life in the wilderness, perhaps among the monastic Essene community that resided near the shores of the Dead Sea. When Jesus approached his thirtieth year, John emerged from seclusion to begin his prophetic ministry near Jericho. It is interesting to note that this is the same area in which Elijah ended his ministry and ascended up to Heaven in a fiery chariot.

By his prophetic preaching, John, like a trumpet, broke the silence that reigned in Israel for nearly four hundred years. Matthew writes in his third chapter, verses 1–3:

> In these days John the Baptist came preaching in the Wilderness of Judea saying: "Repent, for the Kingdom of Heaven is at hand, for this is he who was spoken of by the prophet Isaiah when he said, 'The voice of one crying in the wilderness; prepare the way of the Lord, make his paths straight.' "

John appeared as an Old Testament prophet dressed in a garment of camel hair with a leather belt around his waist, eating locusts and wild honey. We assume the honey was used as a dip for the locusts! People came from all over to hear John preach because they sensed he was an inspired prophet. Their hearts were moved by the Holy Spirit as he called them to repentance; they responded by confessing their sins and being baptized by John in the Jordan River. It is worth noting again that John *began* his ministry near where Elijah *ended* his.

However, an emotional discussion arose among John's listeners as to who John is: Is he Elijah, or is he perhaps the Messiah or some other prophet? John was quick to point out that he was neither Elijah nor the Messiah, but there would be a person coming after him, who was now present, who was far greater than he. This one would baptize them, not with water, but with the Holy Spirit and fire. Today some would have us believe that John preached only hellfire and damnation. Wrong! Luke tells us that he preached *good news* to the people (Luke 3:18).

The good news arrived shortly in the person of Jesus, who appeared with John's listeners by the Jordan. Upon seeing Jesus approaching, John announced with excitement, "Behold the Lamb of God that takes away the sin of the world" (John 1:29). Jesus, who knew no sin, surprisingly asked to join the sinners in baptism. Although John was reluctant to baptize Him because he knew Jesus was righteous, he finally consented. As Jesus came up out of the water, the Holy Spirit descended upon Him like a dove, and a voice from Heaven was heard to say, "You are my beloved son, with you I am well pleased" (Mark 1:11). Some have questioned why Jesus joined the sinners in baptism. Could the reason be that Jesus, even at this early stage, was already bearing our sins for us?

Let us pause for a moment to reflect on what had just happened. John came as a transitional prophet between the Old Testament and the New. By preaching and baptizing near the Jordan where Elijah had ended his ministry and prophecy, John subtly tells us that there is an unbroken relationship between the Old Testament prophets, himself, and Jesus. He is also introducing to us the One to whom all the prophets have pointed. In essence John is saying, "The Master Prophet is now standing among you." All who were present that day were witnesses to the fulfillment of history and prophecy. Jesus left the Jordan River and was driven by the Holy Spirit into the wilderness to be tested, tried, and prepared to be the Prophet. A cave still stands in the mountains near Jericho where it is thought Jesus resided for the next forty days of fasting and prayer. This site may be visited today.

Even today's Navy Seal Team training cannot be compared to the physical, psychological, emotional, and spiritual testing that Jesus underwent in the wilderness. It was a crucible beyond anything we are likely ever to experience. When He emerged victorious over Satan's temptations and God's testing, holy angels aided in His recovery. Then, and only then, Jesus went forth as a prophet, preaching the good news of the Gospel. Certainly, He is God's Son, the Messiah, the coming King and High Priest. However, while engaging in His earthly ministry He took the form of the Master Prophet.

Jesus then moved north to the Sea of Galilee and the territory of Zebulon and Naphtali. This fulfilled the prophecy of Isaiah who said, "The land of Zebulon and the land of Naphtali, the way of the Sea beyond the Jordan . . . the people dwelling in darkness have seen a great light, and those dwelling in the region and shadow of death, on them a light has dawned" (Matthew 4:15–16). We cannot ignore Isaiah's allusion to the powerful light of Jesus shining upon the people.

Jesus proudly confirms His God-given role as a prophet in at least four unmistakable passages. First, in Mark 6:1–4, while visiting His hometown synagogue in Nazareth, He was asked to read the lesson from the Book of Isaiah, which He did. After reading the passage, He sat down to teach, saying that this passage was being fulfilled in their hearing that very day and that a prophet was not accepted in his hometown. He then proceeded to speak about Elijah the prophet. The people, being perceptive, understood that He was comparing Himself to the prophets. This angered the listeners even more, and they rose up to harm Him and cast Him out of the synagogue. It is clear that Jesus was announcing to His fellow citizens of Nazareth that although He has lived among them for thirty years and worked among them as a carpenter, He was actually the Prophet spoken of in scripture.

Second, the next witness Jesus gave to His role is found in Matthew 17 and Mark 9 that record His transfiguration on the mountain in the presence of Peter, James, and John. Although the mountain is not named in the text, it is thought that it is probably Mount Hermon, to the north of the Sea of Galilee, or Mount Tabor, located southwest of the Sea. It is recorded that while on the mountain, Jesus was visited by two heavenly personalities: the prophets Moses and Elijah. The disciples witnessed this and afterward heard a voice from Heaven commanding them to listen to Jesus. The voice seemed to be telling them that although they heeded Moses and Elijah in the past, they must now listen to the superior voice of Jesus the Prophet.

A third witness occurred when Jesus said in Luke 13:33, "I must go my way tomorrow and the day after for it cannot be that a prophet should perish away from Jerusalem." He not only referred to Himself as a prophet but revealed that His death as a prophet must occur in Jerusalem.

Finally, when Jesus encountered the woman at the well in Samaria, the fourth witness occurred. Here Jesus engaged the woman in conversation and, although He had never met her before, He described her life and the number of husbands she had had. She was astonished and replied to Him, "I perceive that you are a prophet of God" (John 4:19). Jesus did not correct her perception.

As we approach the end of this section, we must again declare the absolute supremacy of Christ over all other prophets who came before or after Him. In Hebrews, chapter one, we are told:

> Long ago, at many times and in many ways
> God spoke to our fathers by the prophets but
> in these last days he has spoken to us by his

son, whom he appointed the heir of all things, through whom he also created the world. He is the radiance of the glory of God and the exact imprint of his nature, and he upholds the universe by the word of his power.

—Hebrews 1:1–3

Additionally, Hebrews 3:2–3 tells us that Jesus is faithful to Him who called Him and is worthy, therefore, of more glory than Moses.

Peter, writing to the church concerning Jesus, says, "And we have the prophetic word more fully confirmed, to which you will do well to pay attention as to a lamp shining in a dark place until the day dawns and the morning star rises" (II Peter 1:19).

John writes:

There was a man sent from God whose name was John. He came as a witness to bear witness about the light . . . He was not the light but came to bear witness about the light. The true light which gives light to everyone was coming into the world.

—John 1:6–9

Luke tells us that as Paul approached Damascus, he was struck down by a powerful light from Heaven and heard a voice saying, "Saul! Saul! Why are you persecuting me? I am Jesus whom you are persecuting" (Acts 9:3–5). Paul, who was destined to be a lesser light himself, submitted then to Jesus, the greater light.

In the early days, lighthouses or illumination towers provided a wonderful but limited light in the darkness. They were often little more than small structures with a flaming pot of whale oil set on top; sometimes a strong wind would extinguish them for a time. Today, however, we have lighthouses that employ state-of-the-art construction, engineering, and technology. They are constructed with superior design, materials, lights, lenses, and reflectors, allowing them to reach long distances far out to sea and in many directions continuously.

Jesus had many things in common with the early prophets who went before Him, but none of them can be compared to His light. These early prophets could not speak all of Christ's words, they could not perform all His deeds, nor could they measure up to His righteousness as the Son of God. In the next chapter, we will consider Jesus' important teaching regarding false prophets.

CHAPTER SEVEN

THE TRUE LIGHT WARNS OF COUNTERFEIT LIGHTS

While Jesus and other New Testament writers spoke of the true prophet's role in the new covenant, Jesus spent a great amount of time warning us of false prophets. A rabbi once told me that there have been twenty or more false messiahs who have arisen among the Jews since Jesus. "By their fruits you shall know them," said Jesus in Matthew 7:15. This implies that false prophets are not easily distinguishable from the true prophets but become known only by our careful observation over time.

The first false prophet would have to be the serpent in the Garden of Eden who, loitering by the Tree of the Knowledge of Good and Evil, waited to ensnare Adam and Eve in his lies. The serpent's sweet-sounding lies and half-truths that flowed from his forked tongue are still being repeated today by his false witnesses. As we noted before, in I Kings, chapters 18 and 19, God sent His prophet Elijah, to challenge the false prophets of Baal who were troubling God's people. Isaiah wrote in his ninth chapter that false prophets were telling the people lies. Jeremiah complained that false prophets not only prophesied lies but they exercised influence over the priests of God. The prophet Micah wrote that false prophets were leading God's people astray but that one day they would have their mouths closed. In Jeremiah 14, Jehovah says to the false prophets, "I sent not these prophets yet they ran; I spoke not unto them, yet they prophesied unto you a lying vision, a divination, and the deceit of their own hearts."

Jesus knew the devil's plan to disrupt and spoil His Word and works. He warned us in Matthew 7:15, "Be aware of false prophets who come to you in sheep's clothing but inwardly are ravenous wolves." In Matthew 24:11–12, He continued, "And many false prophets will arise and lead many astray . . . the love of many will grow cold." Also, in Mark 13:22, Jesus said, "For false christs and false prophets will arise and perform signs and wonders to lead astray, if possible, the elect. Be on guard for I have told you these things."

These warnings of Jesus against false prophets are affirmed by the other New Testament writers who followed Jesus. In Acts 13 it is recorded that on the Mediterranean island of Cyprus, Paul and Barnabas met a Jewish false prophet named Bar-Jesus. The false prophet sought to hinder a government official from accepting the Gospel of Christ. When Paul sensed what he was doing, he denounced the prophet as "Son of the Devil, an enemy of righteousness, full of deceit." Paul then blinded Bar-Jesus, and God opened the eyes and heart of the official to become a believer.

However, the most powerful teaching Jesus gives us regarding false prophets who will appear in the Last Days, is found in Jesus' book of prophecy known to us as The Revelation to John. Jesus delivered this powerful, prophetic message to His servant John, while John was exiled on the Island of Patmos. The prophecy focuses primarily on the battle the church was then having and will also have in the future with the false prophets. John saw a vision of the living and powerful Christ and fell at Jesus' feet in total submission. Christ responded, "Fear not. I am the First and Last, and the Living One. I died and behold I am alive forever more and I have the keys to death and Hades" (Revelation 1:17ff.). This vision seems to have been given as an assurance to John of Christ's total victory over false prophets.

If we are to battle false prophets successfully, we too need a clear vision of Christ, lest we become discouraged and confused by false religious leaders. In chapters two and three, Jesus shared His evaluation of His seven churches in Asia, which seem to represent typical churches in every age. All seven churches were battling false prophets at some level. To the church at Thyatira He said, "I have this against you—you tolerate that woman Jezebel who calls herself a prophetess . . ." (Revelation 2:20). He went on to tell the church that He knew that she was teaching and seducing His servants to practice sexual immorality. And who is this Jezebel? A false prophetess in sheep's clothing. Jesus tells them that if she did not repent He would judge her and her children, and they would die. His message to Thyatira was clear and uncompromising: they were not to tolerate false prophets' teaching, leading, or preaching in His church.

As Christ unrolls the scroll of history before us, He reveals the gathering darkness and tribulation. As we read on in Revelation, we see a dark shadow beginning to fall across the world's civilizations, shutting out the true light. This, Christ emphasizes, will be a terrible time of suffering for many. One writer refers to this period as hell on earth. Christ points out that Satan is making one last desperate attempt to assume full authority over God's earth. Part of his plan will be to set up a false trinity to oppose the true and Holy Trinity. Satan will present himself as Father, the antichrist will present himself as God's Son, and the false prophet will present himself as the Holy Spirit. This will be a trinity of deception, lies, and corruption, which will result in terrible suffering for all true Christians. False prophets will use a powerful combination of religion and commerce to control their subjects.

The people will be deceived at first and tempted to follow the unholy trinity that will promise to provide them world peace and globalization. However, when people take the antichrist's mark of 666 (which some have characterized as Sick! Sick! Sick!), they will find themselves entrapped, having denied Christ who is the True Light, True Prophet, and *only* Savior of the World. To oppose the unholy trinity and refuse his mark will mean certain death to many believers. For details of this awful period, the reader is directed to Revelation, chapters 12–19. The glorified Christ, who is the true Prophet, Priest, King, and Savior, will then begin to dismantle the unholy trinity and false prophets with their world power structures. He does so with His wrath because of the harm and damage these false leaders will have done to God's world and God's people. Next, He will cast Satan and all his false followers into the Lake of Fire.

As we contemplate these future events, which are certain to come on the earth, what must the church be doing now to prepare for that day? What religious practices, teachings, disciplines, and structures should we be working on now in order to meet this final challenge? How many antichrists, how many Jezebels, and how many Babylons are we tolerating among us today, simply to keep the peace? Jesus does not call us to take up fleshly weapons against Jezebel and the false prophets, but neither does He approve of our putting these counterfeits on our church boards, teaching staffs, leadership teams, or in His pulpits. How long has it been since we have heard a church leader warn us clearly against the deception of false prophets? We need to urge every Christian and church to embrace the lordship of Christ without reservation and open our lives and His church to His presence and His true prophets.

CHAPTER EIGHT

PROPHETS IN CHURCH HISTORY

To understand something of the church's prophets, we need to look at our church history. Certainly, the apostles, St. Paul, and others were observers of Jesus' prophetic ministry, and were trained by Him. Paul wrote in Ephesians 4:11 that Jesus gave some to be apostles, some prophets, some evangelists, and some pastors. If the order means anything, prophets are listed second after the apostles.

In Acts 21, we have the account of the prophet Agabus who came down from Judea to visit Paul, who was staying with Philip the Evangelist. The prophet came to deliver Paul a message from God. Taking Paul's belt, he bound him hand and foot and then said, "Thus says the Holy Spirit, 'This is how the Jews at Jerusalem will bind the man who owns the belt and will deliver him to the Gentiles.'" Paul's companions urged him to listen to the prophet and not go up to Jerusalem, but Paul did not listen. He went to Jerusalem. Sure enough, Paul was bound by the Jews and given over to the authorities. Which prophet was right—Paul, Agabus, or both? Perhaps both were right, and it was all of God's doing.

Around AD 35, Stephen was martyred as a prophet. As he faced death, he addressed his accusers, telling them in Acts 7:51–52:

> You stiff-necked people, uncircumcised in heart
> and ears, you always resist the Holy Spirit.
> As your fathers did, so do you. Which of the
> prophets did your fathers not persecute? And
> they killed those who announced beforehand
> the coming of the Righteous One whom you
> have now betrayed and murdered.

This enraged the crowd, which set about to stone him to death. We see that Stephen considered himself a prophet, and he certainly allowed the light of Christ to shine through him into the dark hearts of his accusers.

In AD 42, the Apostle James was beheaded by Herod Agrippa, and Nero set in motion a terrible persecution of the church. In AD 65, both Peter and Paul, two of the greatest prophets after Christ, were executed for their prophetic messages. The Roman Emperor Diocletian, in AD 303, ordered a harsh edict, calling for the persecution of the church. Other prophets such as Simeon, a relative of Jesus and Bishop of Jerusalem, were killed, followed by others such as Polycarp, the Bishop of Antioch.

The AD 303 Roman edict further called for churches to be destroyed, sacred writings burned, Christians to lose their civil rights, clergy to be imprisoned or killed, and the believers who would not sacrifice to pagan gods to forfeit their lives. As a result, prophets were no longer welcome in the Roman Empire. Apparently, the Emperor feared the spreading of Christianity's powerful influence over the Empire.

In 324 AD, Constantine defeated his enemy and became the sole ruler of the Roman Empire. Upon doing so, he issued his religious edict, granting tolerance to Christianity. He was baptized a Christian himself, which some have questioned as being simply political; nevertheless, the church and the prophets welcomed their new freedom. In the centuries that followed, the Lord called forth a number of courageous prophets. Among them were Martin of Tours, a soldier turned monk who preached Christ and spread the early monastic movement; Ambrose, Bishop of Milan, a courageous preacher who called for higher moral standards in the church as well as forcing an emperor to repent of the slaughter of the people of Thessalonica; Augustine, a powerful beacon and voice for God out of Alexandria, Egypt, who preached and penned his classics *Confessions* and *City of God*; and Jerome, a lighthouse for God, who was both a powerful preacher and a Bible translator, responsible for creating the *Vulgate,* a Latin translation.

Perhaps the greatest prophet of his time was John Chrysostom, AD 359–407. He was given the name Chrysostom, which means *golden mouth,* 150 years after his death to acknowledge his exceptional preaching. Because of his long, thin frame and his sunken cheeks and eyes, he referred to himself as *the spider.* John was a student under Libanius, one of the most brilliant pagan teachers of that day. Libanius taught Chrysostom from all the philosophers up to that time. Although Libanius never became a Christian himself, Chrysostom did. The teacher considered that Christianity stole Chrysostom from him.

When John became a Christian and was ordained, he did not deny reason but was quick to point out its limitations as opposed to the truth of the Scriptures. As a true prophet of God, he condemned the false prophets of his day and the corruption they brought on the church. John loved the literal interpretation of the Scripture and today would be considered an evangelical. People gathered in great numbers to hear his challenging and thoughtful sermons.

He often quoted from the philosophers, comparing their words to Scripture. He was famous for chiding Greece by saying, "Where now is Greece . . . where the name of Athens? Where the ravings of the philosophers? He of Galilee . . . the uncouth rustic has overcome them all." Although Chrysostom was a gifted thinker and speaker, he nevertheless taught the church to spend time in silence before God before daring to speak for Him. He was a true beacon of divine light and advanced the church spiritually in his day.

Let us now soar all the way to the thirteenth century and consider an earthquake revival that will change the church forever. It was a powerful movement led primarily by prophets. John Wycliffe, an Oxford graduate in England, answered the call to be a clergyman-prophet. He began to speak courageously against what he believed God called corruption in the church. At the time the Vatican, already a wealthy institution, was taxing the English Church, which was short of resources. Wycliffe denounced the tax, but his preaching did not end there; he also announced the supremacy of Scripture over the Pope and the church. In addition, he denounced indulgences in the church. An indulgence was an official written remission for all or part of one's sins in this life and in purgatory after death. These were issued by the church upon the pope's approval and often sold to raise money for the pope's projects.

Wycliffe also started a discussion about the validity of the Doctrine of Transubstantiation. The term *transubstantiation* was the church's doctrine which said that at the words of consecration by the priest, the communion bread and wine are changed into the real body and real blood of Christ, although their appearance remains the same as before. His beliefs could be summarized in these simple words: Trust wholly in Christ; rely altogether on his sufferings; and beware of seeking to be justified any other way except by his righteousness.

Wycliffe believed strongly that all Christians should have access to Scripture in their own tongue and thus set about to translate the Bible into English. The Pope and his Cardinals detested him, but his prophetic voice continued to reach the Vatican. He died before church authorities could bring him to trial and extinguish his light. Because of their disdain for him, Wycliffe's enemies later dug up his body and burned it, casting the ashes into the nearby river. Some said that this made it possible for Wycliffe's message to flow out to the oceans of the world along with his ashes. Wycliffe, as a prophet of God, had lit a light that was destined to spread far beyond England, and no human could stop it.

Wycliffe's light was soon to illuminate another prophet by the name of John Huss of Bohemia in what is now the Czech Republic. The world seemed unprepared for the appearance of this incendiary fourteenth-century prophet. Huss not only spoke like a prophet but looked like one with his long, narrow face, sharp features, and deep, piercing eyes. He was a person one would remember long after meeting him. As a young man, he spent his last cent on an indulgence, receiving a certificate granting him forgiveness of his sins. Entering the University of Prague, he lived a life of poverty. He told an interesting little story of making a spoon out of his small piece of bread in order to eat his few peas; then after eating his peas, he also ate his spoon. Later Huss became the priest at Bethel Chapel in Prague and fell under the influence of John Wycliffe's writings. Just as Huss began to think like Wycliffe, the Pope promoted a large-scale selling of indulgences in Bohemia, the profits of which he would share with the Bohemian king.

When churches began to sell these indulgences, Huss protested publicly, saying that the money would go to support brothels, taverns, and priests living with their girlfriends. He called for a boycott of all such sales and the Archbishop of Prague immediately called for him to explain his actions. The Archbishop demanded that Huss recant his sermons against the church's practice, but Huss responded, "Shall I keep silent? God forbid . . . it is better for me to die than not oppose such wickedness . . ."

As a result, Huss was tried by the church and pronounced guilty. Again, he was asked to recant or die. He chose to die as a true prophet rather than continue as a compromising churchman, asking only that he be burned at the stake publicly rather than in private. In answer to this request, the authorities first dressed him in his priestly vestments and then tore them from his body, defrocking him. Then, placing a paper miter on his head with a picture of three demons on it, they spoke these words over him: "We commit your soul to the Devil." Huss was then paraded through the streets to the site of execution where he was bound to a stake, the fire was kindled, and hundreds of men, women, and children witnessed his agonizing death. His final words were, "Jesus, Son of the Living God, have mercy on me," as the flames rose around his body, snuffing out his life. This great lighthouse was destroyed, but the light of his life and words would travel on into the darkness.

One who would be touched by the lights of Wycliffe and Huss was a monk by the name of Savonarola of Florence, Italy (1452–1498). He answered God's call to become a prophet in the spirit of Elijah. Even as a youth, he was brokenhearted over the sins of Florence, the church, and the world. He prayed and wept over the lewdness, luxurious living, and lack of compassion of the church leaders. He could be seen lying for long periods of time on the altar steps of the church, praying about the sins of his time. Dr. Wesley Duewel, in his book *Revival Fire,* calls him an Old Testament prophet in a New Testament world.

At the age of twenty-two Savonarola wrote a paper entitled *Contempt for the World*, in which he likened the sins of his age to Sodom and Gomorrah. Entering a monastery, he waited for God to call him to his mission. When he began to preach Spirit-filled messages, revival broke out in Florence. One prophecy in particular elicited a strong reaction—that the Pope, the city ruler, and the King of Naples, would all die within a year. Within a year they did! The great Florence Revival that followed results in reforming the entire city right down to the government and the man in the street.

People stopped reading vile books, looking at wicked pictures, and abusing one another. They burned their abominable books and paraphernalia in a large public bonfire. Children marched from house to house singing hymns, calling for people to repent and empty their houses of sinful items. Can you imagine the bonfire that would be required to cleanse an average city in America today? We are beginning to understand why prophets are necessary for the church and the world. They help purify us and move us forward into righteousness.

The church officials were enraged at the prophet. They incited a mob against him, battering down his door, capturing him, tormenting him, and putting hot coals on his feet; yet Savonarola refused to deny God's message he was called to deliver. Finally, he was dragged from his cell and executed. However, the light that he had shone into their darkness as a prophet could not be extinguished.

A German priest by the name of Martin Luther would find himself in that light. The example of these great prophets led to and served as an inspiration for both the Protestant and Catholic Reformations, which transformed the church in the ensuing years. Other mighty prophets rose up after Martin Luther, men of God, such as John Calvin, John Knox, John and Charles Wesley, Jonathan Edwards, Charles Finney, Dwight Moody, the Grahams (Billy, Anne, and Franklin), and many others.

We give God thanks for all these mighty prophets He has given us, but we need many more today as the shadows are again lengthening. More than ever, we need to pray that Peter's prophetic quotation from Joel will be fulfilled: "Your sons and your daughters shall prophesy . . . even on my male servants and my female servants. In those days I will pour out my Spirit and they shall prophesy" (Acts 2:17–18). Is this not God's longing for more prophets today?

CHAPTER NINE

WHERE ARE THE PROPHETS TODAY? SIX VIEWS

A re there prophets today? If so, what forms do they take and what should be our relationship to them? If one thinks that all religious people agree on the answers to these questions, one would be greatly mistaken. Let us now consider six of the most prominent views regarding prophets today:

View of the Jewish Community

The Jewish community differs greatly in their religious beliefs and practices, but they all share a high view of prophets, both past and present. For example, the late Rabbi Meir Kahane was considered a prophet by many because of his zeal for Israel and his warnings about the nation's relationship with Arab nations. He was arrested a number of times for overstepping government lines but maintained a committed following. Now that Arab tensions with Israel have increased, graffiti writing is appearing on Jewish walls saying, "Kahane was right!" Two prominent Israeli women, Tzvia Sariel and Nadia Matar, are also considered by some to be prophetesses.

What qualifies them for this role is their work, promotion, and speeches on behalf of preserving the Holy Land for the Jews.

However, the most honored and renowned Israeli rabbi and prophet in recent years is Yitzhak Kaduri. The Rabbi was born in Baghdad but migrated to Israel at age seventeen. He died a few years ago at the ripe old age of 108. Kaduri had a photographic memory and devoted his entire life to the study of the Torah and prayer for Israel. Not long before his death, he announced to his synagogue on Yom Kippur, the Day of Atonement, that he had met the Messiah. The Messiah's name, he announced, would be written down and placed in a sealed envelope to be opened after his death. When he died, the envelope was opened and inside was the name *Yehashua,* a Hebrew form of the name *Jesus.*

The Jewish media paid very little attention to this shocking revelation; however, it was published on Kaduri's web page and reported in the magazine *Israel Today.* On the other hand, his son, who is also a rabbi, denied that the envelope and name ever existed. One Israeli responded by simply saying, "So he became a Christian." Since then, author Carl Gallups wrote about the Yitzhak Kaduri controversy in his book entitled *The Rabbi Who Found Messiah: The Story of Yitzhak Kaduri and His Prophecy of End Times.* A movie has also been made about the prophecy. Although there may be controversy in Israel over this prophecy, 200,000 people turned out to honor the prophet in the funeral procession to his burial site.

View of the Muslim Community

We now consider Islam and the views of its followers on prophets today. This religious faith boasts a billion-plus followers. Since Islam is not a part of Christianity, I first questioned whether I should include it in our study; however, in my research, I discovered that in recent years 138 Muslim clerics have written letters to Christian leaders, seeking dialogue on peace. Some Christian leaders responded through a letter drafted at Yale Divinity School. This letter, reportedly drafted by Joseph Cummings, director of the school's Reconciliation Program, included an apology for the sins of Christians both past and present toward Muslims. It is said that the letter referenced the one God worshipped by Christians and Muslims alike. Some three hundred Christian leaders signed the letter, including members of the National Association of Evangelicals and Rick Warren, pastor of the Saddleback Church. However, there were other Christian leaders such Dr. Albert Mohler, well-known president of the Louisville Baptist Seminary, who took issue with the letter seeming to equate Allah with the Christian God, Jehovah. Many other Christian leaders agreed with Mohler on this.

We should remind ourselves that according to the Muslim faith, *there is no God but Allah and Mohammed is his prophet.* Muslims recognize Jesus as a prophet but not *the* Prophet. They consider Mohammed to be the Prophet. Although Mohammed acknowledged Jesus as a prophet, he considered himself to be a superior prophet to Jesus. As long as this view continues, there is little room for common-ground dialogue based on the one true God.

View of the Church of Jesus Christ of Latter-Day Saints

According to the LDS Church, or Mormons, as they are commonly known, there is but one true prophet—the president of the Mormon Church. Their view is worth our consideration because this church is highly influential around the world with approximately 16 million members and growing steadily. They also dominate one entire state in our country and because of their sheer numbers and wealth have considerable power religiously, politically, and economically.

In their book *Our Heritage, A Brief History of the Mormon Church,* it is stated that on the evening of September 21, 1823,

Joseph Smith was praying for the Lord to forgive him for his youthful follies and give him further direction. Three years later, according to his writings, the Lord answered that prayer and sent him a heavenly visitor:

> He called me by name, and said unto me that he was a messenger sent from the presence of God to me, that his name was Moroni (a former prophet on earth), and that God had work for me to do and that my name should be had for good among the nations, kindreds, and tongues . . . He said there was a book deposited ,written upon gold plates, giving an account of the former inhabitants of this continent . . . He said the fullness of the everlasting gospel was contained in it, as delivered by the Savior to the ancient inhabitants. (Page 5)

According to Smith, Moroni was the last prophet to write on these ancient gold plates and, as directed by the Lord, he buried them in the Hill Cumorah. Also buried with them was to be the Urim and Thumim, which were the keys to be used in translating the writing. In September 1827, Moroni is reported to have given Smith the golden plates and told him to begin the translation.

About the same time, he also told Joseph that the revival the New York churches were experiencing in his area was all in error. Not only was the revival in error, but also were the churches, the pastors, the evangelists, and even their Bible. At this same time, Joseph Smith claimed to be designated by Moroni as the true prophet of God upon the earth and directed to create a new church, new scriptures, new teachings, and a new book called the Book of Mormon. The latter was meant to be a companion scripture to the King James Bible, which Joseph Smith was also instructed to correct. He translated the Book of Mormon but failed to rewrite the King James Bible, a major failure to follow the divine plan that has never been explained.

Smith claimed his revelations continued, one of the most profound being a personal visitation by Peter, James, John, and John the Baptist. All came to testify that he (Joseph Smith) was the true prophet, called to lead the new church. As his religious movement grew, so did his opposition. Joseph was arrested and jailed but then released. This motivated him and his followers to pick up and move. They ended up along the Mississippi River near Navoo, Illinois, where they settled, built a temple, and sent out missionaries to convert unbelievers. Again, persecution followed them. Smith and a party of followers now set out for Carthage, Illinois, where he was soon arrested and jailed. Two hundred men with painted faces stormed the jail, killing Joseph Smith and his brother Hiram.

The new president and leader of the Mormons paid this tribute to Joseph Smith:

> Joseph Smith, the prophet and seer of the Lord, has done more, save Jesus only, for the salvation of men in this world than any other man that ever lived . . . He lived great, he died great in the eyes of God and His people; and like most of the Lord's anointed in ancient times has sealed his mission and his works with his own blood . . . (Page 65)

The Mormon prophets and their church have accomplished many noteworthy and good things, but it seems evident from critical study that they are in major error. When anyone claims to have the true prophet, the true church, the true teaching, and the true Scripture, there is little room for error. There are a number of serious questions about the church's historical

71

and prophetic claims. But so far, the LDS church shows little interest in opening these boxes for further study.

View of the Roman Catholic Church

In 1870, the Vatican Council met in Rome and defined the doctrine of the infallibility of the pope as follows:

> We teach and define that it is a dogma divinely revealed that the Roman Pontiff, when he speaks ex cathedra, that is, when in discharge of the office of pastor and doctor of all Christians, by virtue of his supreme Apostolic authority, he defines a doctrine regarding faith and morals to be held by the universal Church, by the divine assistance promised him in blessed Peter, is possessed of that infallibility with which the divine Redeemer willed that His Church should be endowed for defining doctrines regarding faith and morals, and that therefore such definitions of the Roman Pontiff of themselves—and not by virtue of the consent of the Church—are irreformable.

The pope is considered as the true Vicar or "agent of Christ," the head of the entire church, the father of all Christians. He is considered the infallible ruler, interpreter of truth—the judge of all—but is judged by no one. This does not mean that the pope is sinless or that he can write Holy Scripture, but it does mean that in his official capacity as head of the Roman church, the Holy Spirit is said to speak through him on all matters of doctrine, faith, and morals. But how does the church know when the pope is speaking *ex cathedra*, or for Christ? Presumably, he would have to tell us.

Since the 1870 Vatican Council, the popes have been slow to claim an *ex cathedra* moment. However, in reality, the faithful within the Roman Catholic Church tend to assume that all the popes' statements and teaching on faith and morals has the authority of Christ. In other words, the pope is accepted as Christ's Vicar and senior prophet. On the other hand, the Bible is silent concerning the doctrine of papal infallibility, and Peter, whom they consider to be the first pope, made no claim for himself. Then why did the Roman Church wait until 1870 to officially define the doctrine? A careful study of church history will reveal that the office of the pope (or senior prophet) was a gradual development. The early bishops of Rome laid no claim to this authority. Therefore, Protestants have traditionally rejected the infallibility of the pope as Christ's Vicar or prophet upon the earth.

View of the Pentecostal-Charismatic (P/C) Movement

This movement generally holds to the view that there are certainly prophets today, but they are found primarily among church movements like their own where the gifts of the Holy Spirit are recognized, welcomed, and practiced. Although they would trace their beginnings to the Day of Pentecost, their American roots can be traced back to the revival that took place on Azusa Street in Los Angeles in the early 1900s. From Azusa Street, this movement grew into a major movement that gave birth to the Assembly of God Church, the Church of God, Cleveland, Tennessee; the Four Square Church; the United Pentecostal Churches; the Vineyard Group; the New Apostolic Reformation Movement; and numerous others. Major names associated with this general movement are Charles Parham, Kathryn Kuhlman, Aimee Semple McPherson, Oral Roberts, Rod Parsley, Bennie Hinn, Jimmy Swaggart, Creflo Dollar, Pat Robertson, Peter Wagner, John Wimber, and Rich Joyner, just to name a few.

One of the unique characteristics of this movement is that they tend to link the prophets' ministry with the Baptism of the Holy Spirit as evidenced by speaking in tongues and often accompanied by miracles, signs, and wonders. This attractive movement has influenced the church far beyond its own faith group in the areas of music, worship style, camp meetings, and healing ministries. People who long for a fresh word from God and concrete evidence of His presence among us are attracted to the P/C movement.

While the recognition and ministry of prophets in these faith groups serve to attract members, energize congregations, and purify the church, there can be a negative side to this approach. The challenge for the P/C movement is to separate the wheat from the chaff. Some understanding is needed concerning how the local church is to assimilate this prophetic ministry so there is not abuse of congregations or individuals.

A clergyman of a P/C denomination told me that his church does not have enough protections in place to avoid all parishioner abuse by false prophets. It is a risk that the church takes in order to welcome prophets into their midst. The P/C movement has a long history of sincerely seeking to experience what the New Testament Church experienced. They have done much good and are one of the fastest-growing faith groups in the Americas—North, South, and Central. Since there is no central church authority to monitor prophets, the monitoring must come primarily from the local church. The difficulty is that the local church is often too weak or reluctant to confront a so-called prophet of God. Therefore, the P/C movement continues to welcome the prophet, which unfortunately, can mean welcoming questionable prophets as well as those who bring genuine blessing to the church. This is an issue with which the church has struggled since its earliest days. This writer himself has observed a number of such abuses.

A first-hand experience occurred while a student at Seattle Pacific College. My preaching class was assigned to visit and observe a worship service different from that to which we were accustomed. I chose to attend Revival Center in downtown Seattle, which had scheduled a series of charismatic speakers. The place was full of what appeared to be working class worshippers the night I attended. The music was lively and loud, and the response was enthusiastic. After the congregation was warmed up, the *prophet* took the podium and announced that he was going to pray for deliverance and healing for those who had taken a faith card the night before. He then invited the card holders to come forward along with the $100 bill they were to bring as a faith offering; they were to stand across the front of the church, holding their offering money over their head.

Around twenty to thirty worshippers rose to their feet, came forward, and held up the money. The healer-prophet came down the line and quickly collected the $100 bills, then went from person to person, laying on hands and saying a brief prayer for each of them. As they were being dismissed to return to their seats, an elderly man arose and walked slowly to the front of the church. He stopped directly in front of the preacher who, somewhat startled, asked him, "Why do you come?" The man, who appeared to be very weak, said he wanted to be prayed for to be healed but had been unable to raise the $100 faith offering. The healer-prophet looked at the man and then spoke firmly to him, "You lack faith. Go back and try to find the $100. If you do, then come tomorrow night, and I will pray for you." The man turned away with a look of despair and shuffled back to his seat. For the first time in my life, I knew I had just seen a false prophet.

Perhaps the worst case of congregational abuse by a false prophet was the massacre at Jonestown Guyana by the notorious Reverend Jim Jones. Rev. Jones had been influenced by some in the charismatic movement but remained independent in his own work. His ministry had begun by helping the needy in Jesus' name, but he began to assume more and more

75

control over the lives of his followers. After a number of years, he began to wield almost total control as their religious leader and prophet.

As part of this control, he acquired land in Guyana, deep in the jungle. Then he led a flock of about 1,000 to that location to live in his communist-like community. They were kept there by armed guards and not allowed to leave. When his California congressman came to check on the welfare of the people, Jones panicked, telling the people they were going to be attacked and killed. He then mixed kettles of Flavor Aid, cyanide, and valium, which he forced the people to drink. The deadly concoction was first given to the babies, then to the children, then to the mothers, and finally to the rest of the group. A total of 912 people drank the poison and died within five minutes. Rev. Jim Jones, their false prophet, died of a self-inflicted gunshot wound to the head.

My Personal View

The sixth view we will consider is the one I arrived at after personal experience, careful study, observation, and prayer. Two personal experiences that shaped my interest in this view occurred at different points in my ministry. The first took place soon after the ship to which I was assigned as Protestant chaplain had returned from a long and arduous deployment to the Mediterranean Sea. The crew was taking leave, spending time with family, and basking in the enjoyment of being back home in Norfolk, Virginia. However, in a few short weeks, the ship received orders to sail to Brazil to train Brazilian pilots in carrier landings. The Christian community aboard the ship was especially upset and prayed earnestly that the ship would not sail. After some time, one of the sailors, a recognized leader in the group, prophesied that God had assured him that the ship would not sail. His Christian brothers rejoiced greatly and were somewhat disappointed when I told them I did not have the same assurance and that we should be careful in announcing such a message. The ship sailed for Brazil on schedule, to the great disillusionment of many in the worshipping community.

The second experience occurred after I retired from the chaplaincy and was appointed to a church. An older man visited me in the church office, inquiring about the views of our church. During the conversation, he volunteered that he had been a self-supported missionary and since returning home had been a part of several churches. In each case, he said, the pastor had asked him to leave for various reasons. I assured him he was welcome to worship with us. However, within a few weeks he came to me again and asked the question, "If I was given a prophecy for your church, would you let me speak it to the congregation?" His question caught me by surprise; I had no time to think through my answer or its implications. After a short pause, I told him that since I was appointed as spiritual leader of this local church by my denomination, I would feel responsible to hear his prophecy first in order to discern if it applied to the congregation and was from God. He bristled in response, saying very firmly, "You have no right to ask that of a prophet." He continued to worship with us, and I came to appreciate his deep and sacrificial zeal for the cause of Christ. He asked no more to pronounce a prophecy to the congregation, and we became good friends. However, his question continued to cause me to ponder the pastor's relationship to a prophet.

Coming from this perspective, this view, in my judgment, is the most biblical, Christ-centered, and consistent with reality. We call this the sixth view not only because it follows the fifth view outlined above, but also because it must fall short of the biblical *perfect number,* seven. None of us should ever claim to have the final and complete interpretation on anything pertaining to the Word of God. The seventh [perfect] view is always His and awaits our full understanding in Heaven.

Here are the foundational pillars upon which our sixth view rests:

1. Jesus said that He fulfilled all that was spoken by the prophets, and Paul declared in Ephesians 2:20 that Jesus was the cornerstone of the apostles and prophets.
2. Nowhere is it recorded in Scripture that Jesus announced the end of the prophets' ministry on earth.
3. We know from Scripture that prophets did exist at the same time as Jesus walked the earth and that they also existed after He departed. However, He was the Master Prophet by which all other prophets must be measured.
4. Paul tells us that Jesus appointed apostles, prophets, and pastors. If order is important here, prophets are listed second only to apostles,
5. Prophets existed in the early church, but the long years of severe persecution took its toll on these early beacons of light.
6. Although the Roman Emperor Constantine lifted the persecution of Christians in AD 313 and was baptized a Christian himself, other issues continued to threaten the prophets.
7. According to Catholic history, Peter was said to be the first Bishop of Rome and the successor of Christ on earth. By the third century, the successor of Christ, now known as the Pope, was considered God's final word (and prophet) for the church. By this time the Roman Catholic Church was organized with Synods ruled by bishops and priests, all strictly accountable to the Pope at Rome. This structure worked against the freedom of the prophets and diminished their voice.
8. Emperor Constantine gave the church considerable resources, money and valuable land, so that by the sixth century the Roman Church had grown to be the largest landowner in the West. The resulting wealth

led to growing corruption in the church. Prophets who tried to speak out against this corruption were brought before the church court and silenced—often by torture and/or death. This did not help in God's recruitment of prophets.

9. The Reformation Movement freed the Protestants from the domination of Rome and gave them the power to restructure their leadership and practices. They no longer had a Pope, so they structured their church around the pastor. This was a great improvement but conspicuously missing was the role of the prophet. While the reformers had openly dissented from Rome themselves, they were not always open to dissenters among their ranks; some of these dissenters were prophets.

10. Although some pastors do function both as pastor and prophet, the two roles are not exactly the same. Over time the position of prophet has been merged into that of pastor and, in my view, has become minimized. The pastoral role tends to dominate today. For example, we hear very little of "Thus saith the Lord," and more primary sources quoted by pastors from other teachers, disciplines, and the Internet. Preaching today is predominately forth telling and little foretelling. The pastor should be open to putting on the prophet's mantle when called of God to do so. It is not one or the other, but the integration of the pastor and prophet will bring revival to the church in these critical times.

11. Prophets were also to trust God for their welfare while pastors are tempted to trust their congregations for their salary, benefits, position, advancement, and security. In some congregations, speaking as a prophet may put these benefits in jeopardy.

12. Finally, our argument for the ongoing ministry of prophets rests also on Jesus' sending the two prophets

in end days as recorded in Revelation 11. The setting of this teaching appears to be near the beginning of the Great Tribulation Period. According to Scripture, this is the beginning of history's darkest hours before Christ returns. In this prophecy Jesus tells us that He will send two prophets into the streets of Jerusalem in the Last Days. It is worth noting that He does not send two priests or two pastors but two prophets who are filled with the Holy Spirit and exhibit great courage. They are given divine powers to not only speak for God but to withhold rain, send forth plagues, and do signs and wonders.

For three and a half years, they prophesy before the world and are divinely kept from harm. They are described as two olive trees and two lampstands. This seems to imply that their message is all about spiritual light—the trees providing the oil for the lamps. At the end of the three and a half years, God's protection is withdrawn from them, and they are murdered, as is often the case with true prophets. The people celebrate their death as if it were Christmas, but God raises them up to life in the street where they have lain for three and a half days. He then calls them up to Heaven in the sight of their enemies.

The Bible says that after their departure from the earth, a great earthquake shakes the city leaving many dead, revealing to them God's wrath over their treatment of His prophets. The departure of the prophets is a profound marker for the church and for the world. After this comes the hand of Christ, with the Tribulation and Judgment. Who are these mysterious prophets and where do they come from? Their names are not given but the description of their power and work gives us a hint. Their ministry is patterned after that of the prophets Moses, Elijah, and Christ. This seems to fulfill the words of Jesus when He said in His parable (Luke 16:27–31) that if someone would not believe Moses and the prophets, neither would they believe even someone who returned from the dead.

In summary, there are many views concerning the role of prophets today. But a careful study will show us that Jesus' plan was for the prophets' ministry to continue to the very end. The darker the night, the more urgent the need for their voices and the light they shine into our darkness. Let us now turn to some solutions to this urgent crisis.

CHAPTER TEN

PREPARING A PROPHET-FRIENDLY CHURCH

- If the day the prophets called The Day of the Lord is near;
- if Daniel's seventieth week of troubled times is approaching;
- if Jesus' prophecy of Matthew 24 is about to be fulfilled;
- if the dark clouds of the antichrist are now gathering on the horizon;
- if the Church Age has but a short time to prepare for the apocalyptic end; then we, like the ten virgins in Matthew 25, should be gathering our oil, trimming our lamps, keeping awake, and watching for the coming of the Bridegroom. In this final chapter, we will present some urgent and practical steps the church and Christians need to take now to prepare for that Day.

1. First, the church must take seriously the biblical teaching on end times. Matthew 24 records that the disciples questioned Jesus about the end of the age. Taking their questions seriously, Jesus provides important teaching in great detail about this period. This issue clearly is not a minor one to Him; however, if you listen to churches today, in many circles you would never know that there

is an end time. The church addresses a myriad of current issues, but prophetic issues are sadly missing.

2. Senior church leaders and pastors must forsake their personal prejudices and fears of putting on the prophet's mantle and start speaking God's hard truth boldly.

3. Church leaders must encourage the younger generation to listen for and respond to God's call to be prophets. Eli the priest helped young Samuel hear and respond to God's call, even though Samuel would later be called to condemn prophetically Eli's own sins.

4. Church leaders and congregations must welcome aboard and make room for the prophets of God, whether they arise from within the church or stand beyond it. Evan Roberts, who was used by God to ignite the great revival in Wales, sought to avoid the church's impulse to control him or make him into a prophetic star. He actually withdrew from the movement, choosing rather to pray for revival in seclusion. The revival, which his prophetic preaching kindled, continued to burn hot across England and the world in his absence.

5. Churches should refrain from any temptation to use their power over pastors to silence or mitigate their prophetic voice. Jesus reminded us that it was the religious people who killed the prophets, not the unbelievers.

6. Churches must welcome both the prophets' foretelling as well as their forth telling. While congregations are conditioned to receive forth telling, they often become uneasy when confronted with the prophets' words of future events. They do not understand that knowledge of the future is a critical part of the Gospel message today. Foretelling gives us a window into what is coming and is meant to motivate our action today. If we remove any consideration of future circumstances, we diminish the urgency of today.

For example, had Jonah spoken to the Ninevites only about their present condition while urging them to repent and change their ways, few would have responded. However, by telling them that they and their city would be destroyed a mere forty days into the future, smiling faces quickly turned sober, attitudes of procrastination suddenly disappeared, and citizens rushed to repent in sackcloth and ashes that very day. This truth may answer why many churches today see little evidence of conviction over sin; perhaps it is because the church is neglecting to proclaim the certainty of coming judgment.

7. Churches should not only hear prophetic preaching from the pulpit but they should also provide prophetic teaching in classrooms, conferences, and seminars for the education and edification of the faithful.

8. The church needs to understand, celebrate, and embrace the prophets in our worshipping communities. As earlier noted, the great lighthouse built at the entrance of Alexandria, Egypt's harbor in the late 200s BC, was one of the Seven Great Wonders of the Ancient World. However, it was not the first lighthouse nor was it the greatest lighthouse. Exodus 24:17 and following tells us that God led the Hebrews to the foot of Mount Sinai where, before their startled eyes, He transformed the mountain into a mighty lighthouse shining into their darkness. It is said that He set the top of the mountain ablaze with the light of His glory and truth. From that great light came the light of the Ten Commandments and our first written Scripture. Turning our eyes forward to the New Testament, we see Christ declaring, "I am the Light of the World." We see His face and garments illuminated as He stood on top of the Mount of Transfiguration. Then turning our attention to the Day of Pentecost, we see flames of fire

resting on the heads of believers, producing a crowd of lighthouses. On this day, Peter stood up to explain what was happening. He declared, "Your sons and daughters will prophesy" (Acts 2:17). According to Peter, their future sons and daughters would be taking their places alongside the prophets of God. This also seemed to be an answer to Moses' prayer, "Oh, that all God's people were prophets" (Numbers 11:19).

9. Churches must welcome back the prophets because they help us save the lost. England's most famous lighthouse, the Eddystone Lighthouse, was built near the city of Plymouth. Prior to the construction of this lighthouse, the pilgrims coming to America—who would plant their own city of Plymouth in America—would have sailed past this dangerous rocky promontory on their way to the New World in 1620. Several years later, after the loss of numerous ships, the new Plymouth lighthouse was constructed on that stone at great risk and sacrifice to the builders. When the beacon was lit, it immediately began to save ships, which were entering and leaving the harbor. However, some years later, a great storm swept down on Plymouth and destroyed the lighthouse. Time did not allow the lighthouse keeper to alert ships already at sea and approaching the harbor. As a result the captain of a fully-laden ship sailing from Virginia to England, expecting to see the light, saw none. Consequently, the captain became disoriented, the vessel veered off course and crashed upon the rocks with devastating results. Only two crewmen survived. This illustrates the importance of keeping the lights burning.

10. True prophets help us identify and expose false prophets before they can deceive us or do us harm.

So, does it matter if we have prophets today? Absolutely!

Conclusion

Throughout history, God has used the prophets as His light-houses of truth. All the early prophets ultimately pointed to the Master Prophet—Jesus the Christ. He was greater than all other prophets and the standard by which all others are to be judged. When He came, He did not end the ministry of the prophets but rather affirmed their work, giving them a vital role in the church until the kingdom of the world has become the kingdom of our Lord and of His Christ (Revelation 11:15).

However, because of a series of circumstances, the church slowly shifted its focus away from prophets and onto pastors. This shift led to the diminishing role of the prophet as well as the diminishing number of prophets, until today few Christians would admit to having heard, seen, or met one. This loss has severely weakened the church and put it at risk. The most critical areas that have been affected are:

1. The area of purifying and correcting the church. This was always a major element in the role of a prophet. Without the prophet's voice, who will call out the church's sins?
2. The area of foretelling, which was always a major contribution by the prophet. By revealing and speaking of future events and the end of the age, the church was motivated to keep focused. In the absence of the prophet, fewer and fewer pastors are willing and able

to answer those who ask, "Tell us when will these things be, and what will be the sign of [His] coming and of the end of the age" (Matthew 24:3).

3. Finally, the area of personal commitment. Mark Hitchcock reminds us in his excellent book *Bible Prophecy* that when Paul unexpectedly met Christ on the Damascus Road and was blinded by His powerful light, Paul's first question was, "Who are you, Lord?" However, his second implied question was, "What would you have me do?" It is easy to ask the first question, but the cost comes in asking the second question. The answer to this question is the key to restoring the prophets and preparing for the last days.

A Prayer

Lord, call me to be a prophet, and I will go.
Call me to feed or house a prophet, and I will do so.
Call me to welcome, to encourage, or to pray for a prophet, and I will obey.
Call me to obey the prophet's message, and I will say,
"Yes, Lord, yes, to your will and to your way."
This I pray in the name of the Master Prophet,
Jesus. Amen.

SELECTED BIBLIOGRAPHY

Arthur, David. *A Smooth Stone.* Lanham, MD: University Press of America, 2001.

Ball, William. *In Search of Life.* Grand Rapids: Baker Books, 1992.

Blackwood, Andrew. *The Prophets, Elijah to Christ.* Grand Rapids: Fleming and Revell, 1917.

Campbell, Joseph. *The Masks of God.* New York: Viking Press, 1970.

Chappell, Clovis. *And the Prophets.* Nashville: Abingdon Press, 1946.

Cook, Joan E. *True Prophets.* Minnesota: Liturgical Press, 2006.

Dolin, Eric J. *Brilliant Beacons.* New York: Liveright Publisher, 2016.

Ford, Kevin G. *Transforming the Church.* Coral Springs, IL: Tyndale House, 2007.

Green, Barbara, ed. *Jezebel, Portraits of a Queen.* Minnesota: Liturgical Press, 2004.

Hamerton-Kelly, Robert G. *The Divine Passion.* Nashville: The Upper Room, 1988.

Hazleton, Leslie. *Jezebel, the Untold Story of a Biblical Harlot Queen.* New York: Doubleday, 2007.

Hitchcock, Mark. *Bible Prophecy.* Wheaton: Tyndale House, 1999.

Jeremiah, David. *Escaping the Night.* Dallas: Word Publisher, 1997.

Knudson, Albert C. *The Prophet's Movement in Israel.* Nashville: Abingdon Press, 2010.

Mays, James L., ed. *Interpreting the Prophets.* London: Fortress Press, 1987.

McKenna, Megan. *Prophets' Words of Fire.* New York: Arbis Books, 2001.

Menezes, J. L. *The Life and Religion of Mohammed, Prophet of Arabia.* Harrison, New York: Roman Catholic Books, 1912.

Miller, John W. *Meet the Prophets.* New York: Paulist Press, 1987.

Our Heritage: A Brief History of the Church of Jesus Christ of Latter-day Saints. Salt Lake City: LDS Church, 1996.

Payne, Barton J. *Encyclopedia of Biblical Prophecy.* New York: Harper and Row, 1973.

Peterson, David, ed. *Prophecy in Israel.* London: Fortress Press, 1987.

Peterson, Jim. *Church without Walls.* Colorado Springs: NavPress, 1992.

Robinson, Darrell W. *Total Church Life.* Nashville: Broadman Publisher, 1997.

Rutz, James. *The Open Church.* Colorado Springs: Seed Sowers, 1992.

Schultz, Samuel J. *The Old Testament Speaks.* New York: Harper and Row, 1990.

Selman, Martin. *Preaching the Prophets.* London: Spurgeon's College Publisher, 2006.

Serenius, Vernon A. *On the Making of Prophets.* Minnesota: Hart Press, 1979.

Sleinke, Peter. *A Door Set Open.* Wheaton: Rowman and Littlefield, Publisher, 2010.

Swindoll, Charles R. *The Church's Purpose, Profile, and Priorities.* Fullerton, CA: Insight for Living Publisher, 1987.

VanGemeren, William. *Interpreting the Prophetical Word.* Grand Rapids: Zondervan, 1990.

Ward, James M. *The Prophet.* Nashville: Abingdon Press, 1982.

———. *Thus Says the Lord, The Message of the Prophet.* Nashville: Abingdon Press, 1991.

Wilson, R. R. *Prophecy and Society in Ancient Israel.* Minnesota: Fortress Press, 1980.

ABOUT THE AUTHOR

E. Dean Cook is a retired Navy chaplain who rose from seaman to captain in a thirty-three-year career. He has also served as a college teacher, college chaplain, director of his denomination's chaplains, and as a senior pastor for ten years. During his leadership as pastor, the church saw rapid growth and was selected by a Lilly Foundation study done at the University of North Carolina as one of three hundred top Protestant churches in America.

He holds a bachelor's degree from Seattle Pacific College, and both a masters and doctorate from Asbury Theological Seminary, as well as an honorary doctorate from Roberts Wesleyan College. His published books include *Salt of the Sea*, *Chaplains: Being God's Presence in Closed Communities*, and *Jonah: A Man Whose Heart and God Were Too Small*.

Dr. Cook now lives quietly with Ruth, his wife of fifty-seven years, in a log cabin along a serene Kentucky stream, enjoying God in His creation and Word.

QUESTIONS FOR FURTHER STUDY

1. Why do you think parishioners prefer the pastoral role of leadership over that of the prophet?
2. Why do you think pastors are often suspicious of present-day prophets?
3. If a person prophesies once or twice, does that qualify them to be called a prophet?
4. Should all prophets be educated, trained, and ordained in order to be credible?
5. Are evangelists the true prophets today?
6. Is there room for prophetesses today?
7. Should prophets be financially supported like pastors, with salaries and benefits?
8. Do you think most churches today are receptive to signs, wonders, and miracles?
9. Should the church help identify and warn against false prophets?
10. If a pastor refuses to exercise a prophetic role in his congregation, should he be confronted by the church?
11. Have you ever attended a class, seminar or conference on prophecy? What was your reaction?
12. Do you think our nation's moral condition is declining and that we could use more prophetic voices?
13. Could people like Jonathan Cahn, author of the best-selling book *The Harbinger,* be an end-time prophet to America? What about Marvin Rosenthal, editor-in-chief of the magazine *Zion's Fire;* or David Reagan, founder and director of Lion and the Lamb Ministries (*Lamplighter Magazine*); or Franklin Graham, evangelist and editor-in-chief of *Decision Magazine.* What do you think they contribute to the prophetic discussion today?

TESTS TO DETERMINE A FALSE PROPHET

1. Does the prophet's life reflect Christ-likeness?
2. Is the prophet's message in agreement with Scripture?
3. Does the prophet call the church and individuals to repentance?
4. Does the prophet exalt Christ's superiority over all?
5. Does the prophet urge the listener to follow after strange gods?
6. Does the prophet focus on money or the prosperity gospel?
7. Does the prophet offer a second book as a companion to the Bible?
8. Do the prophecies of the prophet come true?
9. Does the prophet tell the listeners what they want to hear rather than what they need to hear?
10. Does the prophet sow confusion and deceit among the people?

THE LIGHTHOUSE

Henry Wadsworth Longfellow was one of America's greatest nineteenth-century poets. He was raised in Portland, Maine, a busy seaport, and observed first-hand the importance of the lighthouse. He also experienced his own personal darkness when he lost his first wife in childbirth and his second wife in a devastating fire that also left him physically scarred. The darkness and storms that engulfed his life must have made him even more sensitive to the light. One of his major poems, entitled *The Lighthouse,* was written in 1850. The poem, which is fourteen verses in length, is ripe with spiritual allusions. It begins with an allusion to God's leading Israel out of bondage with the use of a light:

> The rocky ledge runs far into the sea,
> And on its outer point, some miles away,
> The Lighthouse lifts its massive masonry,
> A pillar of fire by night, of cloud by day.

Verse nine speaks of the trustworthiness of the light, and this reminds us of John's words about the light of Christ which cannot be extinguished:

> Steadfast, serene, immovable, the same
> Year after year, through all the silent night
> Burns on forevermore that quenchless flame,
> Shines on that inextinguishable light.

Verse eleven speaks of the testing and trials of the lighthouse which echoes the ministry of the prophets:

> The startled waves leap over it; the storm
> Smites it with all the scourges of the rain,
> And steadily against its solid form
> Press the great shoulders of the hurricane.

As Scripture reminds us, some would be drawn to the light but instead of surrendering to it will dash themselves upon it and die:

> The sea-bird wheeling round it, with the din
> Of wings and winds and solitary cries,
> Blinded and maddened by the light within,
> Dashes himself against the glare and dies.

Verse thirteen speaks of the motive for the lighthouse which is our love for the imperiled mariner:

> A new Prometheus, chained upon the rock,
> Still grasping in his hand the fire of Jove,
> It does not hear the cry, nor heed the shock,
> But hails the mariner with words of love.

It is because of the lighthouse that we have the freedom to live our lives for God and one another:

> "Sail on!" it says, "sail on, ye stately ships!
> And with your floating bridge the ocean span;
> Be mine to guard this light from all eclipse,
> Be yours to bring man nearer unto man!"

CPSIA information can be obtained
at www.ICGtesting.com
Printed in the USA
FSOW01n1416011117
40628FS

9 781545 616055